Remarkable People

By Rob Mordor

Compiled 1 January 2023
Copyright © 2023 Rob Mordor.
All rights reserved.

No part of this book may be reproduced, or stored in a retrieval system, or transmitted in any form or by any means, electronic, mechanical, photocopying, recording, or otherwise, without express written permission of the publisher.

Cover Design by: Rob Mordor

The Villainy Team:
Rachel Gatland, Frances Shingles-Bryant, Adam Charter, Claire Phipps
http://www.facebook.com/groups/TopVillains

All images herein are either public domain or taken by the author.

FOREWARD

On this fragile pale blue dot. Suspended in a sunbeam, is a multitude. A seething mass of humanity that ebbs and flows, and clashes and crashes, forging history, and fuelling foment. A swirling dichotomy of ideals, actions, truth, apathy, wonder, greed, power, corruption, and curiosity.

Humanity is unceasingly diverse, yet as people we will frequently share a common bond... holding fast to hopes and dreams... wanting more for our children than we had ourselves. With each new dawn, we set forth to forge a new path, set sail towards a new horizon, and fly to new lands on the fragile gossamer thread of our own ridiculously curious nature.

We falter and stumble, fail to learn from past lessons, but slowly – perhaps *too* slowly – we move forward. Even if most of us have trouble agreeing which direction 'forward' actually is.

We are strange and unpredictable, irascible, kind, contemptuous, patient, ignorant, and enlightened, and at times our actions as a species may be difficult even for us to comprehend. Yet it is this very strangeness that adds to the wonder of humanity. Each of us brings to the world our own unique blend of strength and weakness, joy and sorrow.

Some of us stand out, however. Not always because we are heroes or villains – though that certainly stands as a factor – but because we were, in some small way, unusual. Remarkable. What follows is a book about some remarkable individuals who had their fifteen minutes of fame, and for good or ill, changed the world around them.

Some of these people you'll likely have heard of… Baron von Richtofen, the World War I fighter pilot… or Edward Teach, the notorious pirate known as Blackbeard… but others will likely surprise you. Not too many have heard of Orestes, the foolish emperor of the Western Roman Empire… or the one-handed knight, von Berlichingen, who raided and sacked caravans across 16th Century Bavaria.

I hope you will read this book – which does not try to take itself seriously – with some enjoyment, and I encourage you to refer to the footnotes as you find them.

I should point out that I'm not a scholar, so it's entirely possible for me to fall into the trap of attributing some information to the occasional dubious source... so if you're reading anything in here you should always proceed with the mindset that "Rob has assumed all care, but no responsibility".

I'm primarily here to entertain, with education as a distant cousin, sitting in the corner, wondering why nobody really wants to play with him. Having said that, I have absolutely no interest in spreading false information... so if I *know* something is dubious or potentially apocryphal, I'll make a point of saying so. Treat everything as "true enough to get you through secondary school", and don't quote me as a primary source, and you'll probably do OK.

As always, I am eternally grateful that people want to read my writing, so consider this my *Thank You*, and please feel free to visit my Facebook group, **Villainy** at http://www.facebook.com/groups/TopVillains

Rob Mordor
January 2023

KING AFONSO IV (1291-1357)

From an age of war and rivalry, the life of Afonso IV was one of brutal Machiavellian intrigue, and violence. You could argue that he was a child of his age, but some things remain beyond the pale.

Afonso was the rightful heir to the Portuguese throne, but his father, King Denis, favoured Afonso's illegitimate brother who, it seems, was rather more regal and kingly in bearing than the legitimate son.

The two were therefore not friends, and Afonso and his half-brother thrust the country into civil war on more than one occasion even while King Denis[1] was still alive. Upon the old King's death, Afonso assumed the throne and had his brother stripped of all lands, money, and titles, and had him exiled to the Iberian Peninsula.

That didn't stop the feud, and there were multiple attempts to usurp the crown until peace was declared by the two... on the insistence of Afonso's mother, Elizabeth of Aragon. Now, so far this just seems like the sort of carry-on that goes on in royal circles. Legitimate heir or not, the half-brothers were likely both just as bad as each other, and both wanted to be king. The real villainy begins several years later, when Afonso's son, Prince Peter, is grown.

Peter was in a politically arranged marriage to Constance of Peñafiel. When she died in childbirth, he took up with her former lady in waiting, Inês de Castro. While he did not cast away his own children, he did recognise de Castro's existing children as legitimate, and his. The problem was that de Castro's family was aligned with Afonso IV's rivals, and he didn't consider her 'noble' enough to be marrying his son.

Peter, on the other hand, refused all attempts to get him to marry 'according to his station'. He wanted Inês de Castro, and no other.

So, Afonso ordered de Castro imprisoned in a convent, in the hope that his son would lose interest in her. When he did not, Afonso had her murdered. Beheaded, in fact, in front of her children. For some reason, he seemed to think that this would calm his son down and set him back on the 'right' path to marry according to political expediency.

As you might expect, this did not sit well with Peter, who - rather than reconcile with his father and marry a princess - put himself at the head of a rather large army and set about wiping out his father's holdings in the top third of Portugal.

The campaign was quite devastating, and the country between the Douro and the Minho rivers in northern Portugal was absolutely devastated.

Peter reconciled with his father in 1357, almost immediately prior to Afonso's death in Lisbon... and I'm almost entirely sure that Peter had nothing to do with it.

When Peter became king, he hunted down the assassins his father had used to kill Inês de Castro, and their hearts were cut out as a symbol of what they had done to him.

So, Afonso ordered de Castro imprisoned in a convent, in the hope that his son would lose interest in her. When he did not, Afonso had her murdered.

JULIA AGRIPPINA (15-59)

Brother of Emperor Caligula, wife of Emperor Claudius, and mother of Emperor Nero, Agrippina was central to the Roman powerbase, and for a short time, one of the most ruthless tyrants the empire had ever seen.

Born in what is now Germany and touring the provinces with her parents - Julia Agrippina first entered Rome at around age five. At age 13 she was married off to a consul called Gnaeus Domitius Ahenobarbus – who was described as "a man who was in every aspect of his life detestable".[2]

It was because of this marriage that Nero[3] would be born, Agrippina's only natural son. In a moment of premonition, Domitus would comment "I don't think anything produced by me and Agrippina could possibly be good for the state or the people".[4]

Emperor Caligula

Agrippina's brother Caligula was emperor at this stage, and he had reportedly gone mad. There was a lot of discontent among the court, and it was only a matter of time before he was forcibly deposed. Agrippina (among others) was involved in a plot to assassinate him, which unfortunately - for them - failed.

Now Caligula's quite the horror story himself. I recommend reading a brief history or two, but be warned that Roman history in general is a rabbit hole, and if you fall down it, you may never get back out.

Rather than kill her, Caligula exiled her to a distant island off the coast and sold everything that she and her husband owned. Domitus - who probably had nothing to do with the plot - died shortly thereafter of disease.

> *One of the reasons I'm not a big fan of Roman villains in general is because they always read a bit like someone's taken a family tree, shaken it up, and then had George RR Martin write the history. If people aren't murdering each other, it's mainly because they're already dead... and it's hard to keep track of all the angst.*

Now... a bit of fortuitous timing, Caligula was

murdered anyway, by someone else, and the new emperor, Claudius, had Agrippina brought back from the islands... but apart from her name, she had little else - as all her assets had been sold off.

Emperor Claudius

She became somewhat brazen in her attempts to secure a wealthy husband, but she steered clear of the imperial court, largely because the wife of Claudius didn't like her very much, and had sent assassins to kill her son, Nero. The assassins failed.

This rather savage wife of Claudius was called Messalina, and she had given Claudius his first son, Brittanicus. The name Messalina is now used as something of an insult, and referring to someone thus is to suggest that she is both devious and sexually voracious.

> *The reason the assassins are said to have failed was because they saw a snake in Nero's room, and thought it was a bad omen. Turns out it was just a shed snakeskin, but it supposedly saved Nero's life.*

While this was going on, Agrippina married, and then poisoned, a wealthy man called Crispus, and gained his estate as a wealthy widow.

By this time, Claudius was widowed (he'd had Messalina executed for trying to kill him) and he elected to marry Agrippina. Given that she was his niece, this was sort-of frowned upon, but... well, when you're ruler of the known world, you basically get to say what's moral and what's not.

It did mean that the union was not well respected within the court, and this alienated Agrippina somewhat. Those who spoke poorly of her, however, soon learned that this was ill-advised. Agrippina quickly consolidated her power by having several of her rivals within the court murdered, and then made plans for Nero to take the place of her new husband, Claudius, as Emperor of all Rome.

The first step was convincing Claudius to adopt Nero as his actual son, securing his rights to the throne. This cast out Brittanicus, the emperor's own son, and in order to help ensure this, Agrippina had the boy's outspoken tutor executed on trumped up charges.

When everything was in place for Nero to take the throne and become emperor, Agrippina poisoned Claudius with a plate of dodgy mushrooms.

Nero became emperor as a result.

Emperor Nero
Because of his youth, this left Agrippina holding the reins of power. She enjoyed great authority at the head of the Roman Empire, until her son began to get a little belligerent and confront her

for making decisions for him.

This left Agrippina somewhat annoyed, and she decided she loved power more than she loved her son, so she courted the lad Brittanicus as a potential successor to Nero.

This naturally worried Nero, and he promptly had Brittanicus murdered, and started to dismantle his mother's power base... slowly depriving her of honours and powers until such time as she was left with little more than some personal wealth and a place to live.

Then she died.

The End of Agrippina

Accounts vary, but the general consensus is that Nero decided he'd had enough.

He had tried poison, and an increasingly complex arrangement of falling ceiling tiles and venomous creatures until - in a twist that would not be out of place in a James Bond movie - he had a self-sinking boat built.

The idea being that Agrippina would be tricked aboard the boat, and then when at sea, it would open its bows and quickly succumb to the waves. This actually worked, but Agrippina didn't drown.

She swam to shore, and made it known that she had survived... which unfortunately, alerted the three assassins that Nero had sent to make sure the job got done properly. Which they subsequently did.

Her tale didn't end there though. Whether you believe in Nero's madness or revenge from beyond the grave, her death was on his conscience, and her ghost is said to have haunted Nero for the remainder of his ill-fated rule.

> *In the end, she was responsible for the deaths of at least 12 individuals on her rise to power. She was very clever, and very politically savvy. She was remarkably ruthless and quick to anger, and one of the most influential women in Roman history.*

ALPHONSE ALLAIS (1854-1905)

Alphonse Allais was a poet, artist, writer, journalist and humourist. Well, that's the official tale. Read on, and you can decide whether you'd describe him this way, or whether you'd choose a more... apt... description.

He's responsible for some legitimate cleverness and had a way with words. He was quite fond of a verse form known as holorhyme, where multiple lines containing different words would be pronounced the same.

For example:

> *Par les bois du djinn où s'entasse de l'effroi,*
> *Parle et bois du gin, ou cent tasses de lait froid.*

Did I mention he was French? Yeah, he's French. So, that bit probably works better if you can read French. Being French doesn't make him remarkable, however... not these days... so why am I picking on Mr Allais? Some of his other artwork and practices were... irritating.

To an exhibit in 1883 he submitted a plain white sheet of Bristol paper, and titled it *Première communion de jeunes filles chlorotiques par un temps de neige* (First Communion of Anaemic Young Girls In The Snow)

The following year in 1884, he submitted a plain red sheet of paper, titled *Apoplectic Cardinals Harvesting Tomatoes on the Shore of the Red Sea*.

He also wrote the earliest known example of a completely silent musical composition, with *Funeral March for the Obsequies of a Great Deaf Man* in 1897, and it consisted of 24 completely silent measures.

> *I mean, yes, he was a humourist... but I'm sorry... this irks me. I'm irked. It's borderline dadaism - albeit predating the concept - and this is something I'd have to admit that I never warmed up to. When he wasn't sending blank pieces of paper to art galleries, Allais was quite fond of chasing the green fairy, and would write a lot while drinking absinthe. He was quite prolific, and it clearly worked for him, because to be fair a lot of his work was (quite rightly) highly regarded.*

All the above would just make me think he was a bit of an irritant and leave it there, so do I have still more to go? Indeed, I do.

Allais would travel extensively for his work, and he didn't skimp on the quality. He would elect to stay at some of the more highly regarded establishments, and because his star was ever rising, they were generally very happy to have him. Furthermore, they would tend to accommodate some of his more outlandish requests... such as his wake-up call.

Instead of requesting a traditional wake-up call, Allais would request that the concierge loudly rouse the rooms on either side of his. So that he could be, and I quote:

> *Gently woken by the sound*
> *of neighbours' protests.*

I cry "Villain!" Mainly, I admit, because I really want to give this a try now.

SAWNEY BEAN (16TH CENTURY – POSSIBLY APOCRYPHAL)

You can't get much more remarkable and horrible than cannibalism, and Alexander "Sawney" Bean - a 16th Century Scottish clan-leader - is said to have eaten over 1,000 people during his 25-year reign of terror. That's only a little less than one person a week, so... he'd been busy.

It's the late 1500s, and King James VI of Scotland, spurred on by horrific tales of cannibalism around the Firth of Clyde sends out search parties to get to the bottom of 'the troubles'. What the searchers find is a cave, and a story fit to chill you to your very bones.[5]

This is scary stuff. If you're reading this at night, turn out the light, spark up an extra-dribbly candle, and huddle under a blankie. Insert woogie-woogie noises at will.

Sawney Bean was born in the South-East of Scotland in the 1500s to a ditch-digging father and hedge-trimming mother. He decided fairly early on that he was not suited to the family trade and took up robbery and thievery instead.

According to legend (and let's face it, this whole tale might be apocryphal) he hooked up with a rather unpleasantly vicious lass called Agnes, who shared his violent inclinations. Together they, became outlaws, living in a cave in Bennane Head between Girvan and Ballantrae.[6]

As well as accumulating children of their own, the two scoundrels had eight sons, six daughters, 18 grandsons and 14 granddaughters. Various grandchildren were products of incest between their children.

Already this is fairly horrific... but this state of affairs lasted for around 25 years. As the cave was hidden during high tide, it was remarkably secure, and the population of the region was low enough at the time that not too many people would have been exploring. Those that were exploring could have been... discouraged.

The family maintained their original occupation of banditry. Sawney and his clan survived by setting up night-time ambushes. They would rob and murder small groups of travellers - preferring those who were clearly not local. They would bring dead bodies back to the secret cave, where they were eaten, with leftovers pickled in barrels for later.

Eventually the body count became rather too much to ignore, even in an age when lifespans were horribly short, and life was cheap. It was a botched attack against an accomplished warrior that ended up being the final nail in the coffin of Sawney Bean and his clan.

Picking on the tail-end of a caravan, Bean and his clan tried to pick off a few stragglers during a moonless night. One of the people they faced, however, was able to hold them off long enough for others to raise the alarm, and the Beans had to vanish into the night.

And we come back to King James VI of Scotland, who upon hearing of the attack, gathered 400 men, several bloodhounds, and sought to lance this cannibalistic boil once and for ever.

Sawney was winkled out of his hidey-hole, and his entire clan was dragged to Glasgow, where they were executed without trial - being seen as subhuman monsters, rather than people.[7]

Some people believe that Sawney Bean was a real person, while others think he was just a mythical figure. There is some compelling evidence that the tale is rooted in fact, however... though the dates and timelines may be confused.

Cannibalism was certainly not unknown in Scotland, though most recorded examples of it were at least a couple of centuries prior to the Sawney legend. It is suggested that the earlier tales were embellished, combined, and made more contemporary in order to be more compelling to readers... in much the same way as the Robin Hood tales.

However you look at it, whether historical fact, concatenated legends, or total fabrication, Sawney Bean is a remarkable person of the first order.

Sawney was winkled out of his hidey-hole, and his entire clan was dragged to Glasgow, where they were executed without trial - being seen as subhuman monsters, rather than people.

HENRY BERESFORD (1811-1859)

Most of you will have heard the phrase "painting the town red" as a way of describing a great night out, usually involving drinking, dancing, and general abandon. Henry Beresford is where the phrase came from.

Beresford was 3rd Marquess of Waterford and lived in England in the mid-1800s. A marquess is a nobleman of high birth indeed. One of the creams of the crop as far as heredity is concerned.[8] Historically, a Marquess would have ruled a moderate area of land, but in the 1800s, it had devolved primarily to become a social rank.

Needless to say, if you were a Marquess, you were well off, and almost certainly had expensive tastes. Henry became the Marquess at age 13, so it's probably no surprise that he turned out to be a bit of a bad egg.[9]

PAINTING THE TOWN RED

At around age 25, Beresford and his fox-chasing chums had been living it up large at the races. They arrived home at the town of Melton Mowbray and demanded to be let in the tollgate.

The tollkeeper refused to let them in without payment. Unfortunately, as the tollgate was in the process of being repaired, there was a lot of paint and timber around... so rather than pay the toll, Beresford and Co. attacked the tollkeeper and painted him bright red.

They then proceeded to paint the gate, a passing constable, and several other members of the public... also bright red. They then continued into town, and really ran amok.

In a running game of "paint everything red", they painted people's front doors, smashed things, and even climbed up to paint statues and signs. Whatever they couldn't paint red, they picked up and threw into the canal.

As individual policemen arrived, Beresford had them seized and painted, and occasionally tossed into the canal. When several turned up at once and arrested one of the rioters, the rest of the rioting fox hunters stormed the local gaol and demanded his release "on pain of murder".

The next day brought recriminations, much tutting, and no doubt several remarkably intense hangovers.

Beresford eventually did sober up, and somewhat grudgingly paid for all the damage... but the whole group were hauled before the courts and ordered to pay £100 each.

Given that the annual wage was in the low tens of pounds back in England during this period, this was a considerable fine. They managed to avoid significant further charges by dint of being extremely wealthy nobility... because you don't just chuck them in prison for rioting if you're a judge in the mid-1800s who knows what's good for him.[10]

The term 'painting the town red' soon entered the British lexicon.

SPRING HEELED JACK
A popular rumour in the 1830s claimed that Beresford was the main suspect behind the "Spring Heeled Jack" phenomenon.

Now, even if you've heard of painting the town red, there's a good chance you've never heard of Spring Heeled Jack. This was an urban legend character from the mid-1800s. A well-dressed and frightening fellow who would spring upon the unwary, terrify them beyond all belief with breath of fire.

The creature would assault them, cause accidents by frightening carriage-horses, light fires, and then vanish with a maniacal cackle, and prodigious leaps and bounding.

> ...*the unmanly villain has succeeded in depriving seven ladies of their senses, two of whom are not likely to recover, but to become burdens to their families. The affair has now been going on for some time, and, strange to say, the papers are still silent on the subject. The writer has reason to believe that they have the whole history at their finger-ends but, through interested motives, are induced to remain silent.*
> *- Written Complaint to the Lord Mayor of London (1838)*

So, why was Beresford a suspect for this rogue? On at least one incident, Spring Heeled Jack was described as wearing clothing embroidered with the fanciful 'W' coat of arms of the Marquess of Waterford, which was, of course Beresford's title. Many of the incidents involving Jack also occurred in proximity to Beresford's estates.

OTHER VILLAINIES

Even if you don't subscribe to the Spring Heeled Jack conspiracies (and that's reasonable) there's plenty of other documentation to demonstrate that Beresford was more than a mere drunken lout:

He once galloped a horse through a busy town, apparently not much caring what injuries he caused by doing so. He was summoned to court for this, and arrived on horseback, and demanded that all questions be addressed to his horse - "for the steed himself can only know how fast he was going."

He took several barrels of gin to a large London market, and handed out free mugs of alcohol to passers-by, with the express intention of causing a drunken riot. He got one. Eventually, everyone got so drunk that a riot broke out and Beresford had to be arrested for his own safety.

He once penned a poisonous little letter to the London and Greenwich Railway Company offering them thousands of pounds if they could see their way to arrange a deliberate train crash for him to observe so he could laugh at the victims.

He died of a horse-riding accident in Ireland in 1859. While he seems to have settled down somewhat in later life, and even if you discount the whole Spring Heeled Jack connotations, here lived a remarkable rogue who seemed far more unpleasant than gloriously eccentric.

GÖTZ VON BERLICHINGEN (1480-1562)

Gottfried "Götz" von Berlichingen (AKA: Götz of the Iron Hand) was a Franconian Imperial Knight, a mercenary, and poet. He was born into the noble family of Berlichingen in modern-day Baden-Württemberg (Western Germany).

Being a mercenary, he was a hero too those with the cash, and a villain to those without. He was active militarily for almost fifty years... which is probably longer than most people lived back in the 1400s.

THE LOSS OF HIS RIGHT ARM

During the 1504 *Siege of Landshut* in Bavaria, Berlichingen had part of his right arm blown off by a cannon. He had two iron replacements made. One was so adeptly built, that it allowed him to hold a quill, a shield, and horse's reins... meaning he could still fight, ride, and write.[11]

He already had a bit of a reputation by this point. His name actually became a euphemism. Berlichingen was euphemiated (I made that up. I'm quite proud of it) into:

Er kann mich am Arsch Lecken

... which is a naughty thing to shout in a nunnery.

However, he went a little out of his way to annoy people who should probably remain... unannoyed.

THE IMPERIAL BANS
He raided a caravan of merchants returning out of Leipzig, and the emperor (Maximilian) placed him under imperial ban. He remained under this ban for a few years. This means he's basically an outlaw.

Berlichingen went through merchants like most folk go through popcorn. They were a relatively inexpensive snack full of empty calories, but oh so tempting.

He was only able to be un-banned after raising a significant sum of money - 14,000 gulden. That works out to roughly US$3 million in today's money. We won't go into how he raised this, because it would probably have been the result of leaning on some debtors and raiding more caravans of merchants.

So, now being un-banned, and a fine upstanding

member of society again, he very quickly got himself back into trouble by raiding a nearby province and capturing a count for ransom. The emperor banned him again.

ONGOING MILITARY CAREER

Even banned, his prowess as a warrior was well-known, and in 1519 he was employed by a Duke who was at war with the Swabians. He was unfortunately soundly thrashed and captured. The terms of surrender were violated, and he was handed over to the inhabitants of a town he had raided several times in the past.

Rather than kill him, they ransomed him for 2,000 gulden... so he was free once more.

REBELLION AND RETIREMENT

The German peasants were revolting.[12] This became known as the *German Peasant's War of 1525*. Berlichingen was employed to lead the rebel army against the princes of the Holy Roman Empire. Money clearly talked, because he was vocally not a supporter of the rebellion.

He actually found the rebels to be too rebellious and had trouble controlling their excesses. Berlichingen deserted his command and holed up in his castle until it was all over. The imperials won, and Berlichingen was locked up once more... being guilty primarily of being linked to the losing side.

Once released - which didn't take too long, really, he was placed under house-arrest in the castle he had bought with all his years of raiding and mercenary...ing... and basically spent his remaining 20 years introducing his liver to a wide variety of different types of quality alcohol.

THOMAS BLOOD (1618-1680)

Take a seat, ladies and gentlemen... this one is a doozy. If you're already seated, the slouch down a bit.

Thomas Blood was born in Ireland of a successful English land-owning blacksmith, and an Irish mother. His family had a good, prosperous reputation. His grandfather was a member of the Irish Parliament.

Blood himself, however, was something of a desperado, and a malcontent.

In the early part of the 1600s, England was rocked by civil war. The Royalists (loyal to King Charles I) were locked in battle against Oliver Cromwell's Roundheads. This was a brutal struggle, which certainly warrants some attention all by itself... but we're focusing on one fascinating little cog in this rather large machine... and that cog, Thomas Blood, moved to England and took up arms with the Royalists.

THE FIRST ENGLISH CIVIL WAR

Blood was no fool, however, and his loyalties were not without negotiation. Seeing which way the cookie was crumbling... that is, that the Royalists were getting their collective backsides handed to them by Cromwell's lads... he switched sides and became a lieutenant in the Roundhead forces.

As a result, once the conflict abated, Cromwell (who liked a good turncoat, as it happens) awarded Blood a decent parcel of land and appointed him a Justice of the Peace... which was quite a powerful position back in the day.

Blood was therefore quite well off, had a bit of power, and was able to lord it up, as was his style. There's not a lot of surviving record about what he did as a Justice of the Peace, but if it didn't involve at least a little bit of carousing and general raconteur, he wasn't doing it properly.

England was not exactly the most stable place to live back in the mid-1600s, and it wasn't too many more years before the restoration, and the reign of King Charles II.

Part of this involved grabbing back land and titles which Cromwell had handed out like candy, and Blood subsequently fled with back to Ireland... all his assets stripped.

THE DISCONTENT IN IRELAND

This did not sit well with our side-swapping

former JP, and as you can imagine. He harboured just a teeny smidge of a grudge. As you would.

He wasn't the only former Cromwellian to run back to Ireland, and he decided he was going to band them all together and cause insurrection, the likes of which Ireland had never seen before.

> *Ireland had seen all sorts before and would see all sorts again. Ireland is historically the place where insurrection went on its holidays to recharge, refuel, and have a bit of a regroup before embarking back out into the world in general. Blood's contribution, in the grand scheme of things, was moderately meagre.*

So, a plan was made to storm the seat of power in Ireland (Dublin Castle), kidnap James Fitzthomas Butler, First Duke of Ormonde, and hold him for ransom.

Blood's plans were foiled, however, and a raid by the authorities just the night before it all kicked off had the band of former Cromwellians scattered. Many were caught and executed, but Blood ultimately escaped to The Dutch Republic (a predecessor to The Netherlands) to hunker down for a while until the heat blew over.

THE DUTCH REPUBLIC'S HIRED GOON

Making himself useful to the locals in power was a good way to stay alive and well-fed. It is believed that Blood fell in with Admiral de Ruyter, an opponent of the English forces in the Anglo-Dutch Wars.[13]

He was subsequently implicated in a few actions against English forces... and possibly even acted as a hatchet man for George Villiers, 2nd Duke of Buckingham, who had many enemies that he was politically unable to deal with directly.

THE ATTEMPTED ASSASSINATION OF ORMONDE

While the Netherlands were all well and good, Blood was not content to lie low for long. Disguising himself, he returned to England pretending to be a doctor, and set himself up in London and kept an eye out for his arch-enemy James Fitzthomas Butler, First Duke of Ormonde.

After watching his activities for a time, Blood and a gang of other thugs ambushed Ormonde, killed his guards, and dragged him from his coach.

They pinned a note to his chest detailing all of his 'crimes', and were going to hang him in Tyburn, in Middlesex, when one of Ormonde's surviving men - brave beyond all reasonable measure - freed Ormonde, and the two of them escaped.

Blood was, as you can imagine, furious, and at this stage, with his plans coming apart like a marshmallow bunny-rabbit at a convention of hungry toddlers, he was at risk of becoming more like Edmund Blackadder than some

Machiavellian Impresario.

However, finally having had enough, Thomas Blood decided that he was going to go right for the big-game and steal the crown jewels right out from under the noses of the Royalty.

THE THEFT OF THE CROWN JEWELS

The heist to end all heists, and certainly something of a staple of speculative crime writers. The crown jewels are the ultimate in treasures... kept in the Tower of London, at the time under the control of the Custodian and his wife.

Blood disguised himself as a parson and ingratiated himself with the Custodian. Becoming firm family friends, he even went so far as to offer up a (fictional) family member in marriage to the Custodian's son, and a dinner party was arranged to accomplish this.

During said dinner party, Blood convinced the Custodian to show the party the jewels in their chamber, and upon doing so, he and his men attacked the Custodian, by sticking a bag over his head, and hitting him with a mallet.

The guy survived and was awarded £300 by the crown for his bravery... though, some may say 'typically'... it was never paid in full.

Blood also used the mallet to flatten *St Edward's Crown* so that he could stuff it up his jumper. An accomplice sawed the *Sceptre with the Cross* in half so that they could fit it in a non-descript bag. A third man shoved *The Sovereign's Orb* down his trousers... beyond the wit of any guardsman to locate, no doubt.

They took too long, however, and a guard happened upon the events as they unfolded. With cries of "Murder! Treason!" and "The crown is stolen!", the plan started to unfurl like a ragged pair of pants with a heavy gold orb stuffed down them.

The conspirators scarpered to nearby horses and took to their heels.

What followed was a running gun-battle across London. Well, a little bit of it. The bag containing the sceptre was dropped... the man with the orb stuffed down his knickers couldn't ride very well, and was quickly captured... and Blood himself, refusing to give up, went down under a hail of fists, clutching a flattened crown, shouting "It was a gallant attempt, however unsuccessful! It was for a crown!"

HOW LUCKY IS THIS GUY?
So, caught, finally, after decades of causing all sorts of trouble in England and abroad. Ormonde was thrilled to bits, expecting to see his nemesis finally brought to justice.

Blood, however, refused to talk to anyone other

than King Charles II... so dragged in chains into court, King Charles asks the man:

What if I should give you your life?

I can imagine Ormonde's jaw hitting the ground at this point, but I can only assume that Charles saw in Blood some kind of heroic desperado, worthy more of song than of hanging.

Blood, clearly not wanting to push his luck too far responded:

I would endeavour to deserve it, Sire!

... and so, he was pardoned.

Not only pardoned but given land in Ireland worth £500 a year. Following his pardon, Blood became a servant of the crown, and made frequent appearances at Court where he was employed as a royal advocate.

THE DEATH OF A REMARKABLE MAN

Blood died on 24 August 1680 at his home in the rather amusingly named Bowling Alley, Westminster. It is speculated, however, that he may have faked his death in order to avoid paying debts owed to the Duke of Buckingham... though being in his sixties in a country that had an average life expectancy of around 40 at the time... it is perhaps, not unexpected.

Blood was not only pardoned but given land in Ireland worth £500 a year. Following his pardon, Blood became a servant of the crown, and made frequent appearances at Court where he was employed as a royal advocate.

BILL BOAKS (1904-1986)

All the world needs a rebel, and LtCom Boaks of the Royal Navy was a rebel and a half. He was a navy man of some repute, and had served his country with distinction during World War II.

Boaks received a Distinguished Service Cross for his actions on board the destroyer HMS Basilisk during the evacuation of Dunkirk in 1940, and was gunnery officer aboard the battleship HMS Rodney, which aided in the sinking of Bismarck in 1941.

He was no stranger to conflict, and both of those engagements were particularly fraught affairs, to be sure. Furthermore, he was amongst the first Allied officers at Nagasaki and Hiroshima after the US dropped nuclear weapons on both.

It's safe to say that he saw things that couldn't be unseen, and which probably haunted him somewhat.

Boaks retired from the Royal Navy in 1949,

shortly after the war. His political aspirations began in earnest in the early part of the 1950s.

During the 1951 general election, he contested Walthamstow East in the UK as an independent candidate for ADMIRAL[14] for which he was the sole member. He received a massive 0.4 percent of the vote and finished dead last.

Realising that he was unlikely to be able to take down the system from within, Boaks decided that he would campaign about things that got on his wick independently, and what was getting on his wick for the most part was traffic in the United Kingdom.

If you're the sort of person who gets stressed about the very idea of having to sit in a queue on a road, consider this a trigger warning.

Due to a shortage of funds, Boaks built an armoured bicycle - which had an iron bedframe welded to it, and which was probably far more dangerous to him than it was protective.

Boaks wanted to cause so much traffic chaos that UK citizens would spontaneously choose to give up their cars and begin travelling by bus or helicopter instead – landing-pads for which he insisted should be installed in cities across the nation.

As well as blocking traffic for extended periods using this contraption, he would also hold up traffic by walking repeatedly across zebra-crossings whilst wheeling a pram full of bricks... or would sit in the middle of major motorways in a deckchair reading a newspaper.

In 1955, right before the start of an England vs Scotland football match at Wembley Stadium, Boaks parked a van outside and refused all attempts to get him to move until every single spectator had crossed the road in front of it. This took ages, and traffic was backed up for miles.

His slogan for his candidature in 1964 council elections was "Public Safety Democratic Monarchist White Resident" - being limited to six words in total.

The racist overtones there are vague, but regrettable, though Boaks himself had gone on record to state that it was in no way a reflection of his feelings towards any other ethnicities, but as a goad to 'left-wingers', who he stated he distrusted immensely - even though many of his own policies were decidedly left-wing.

Boaks apparently became one of the first outspoken promoters of ethnic minority candidates in UK elections, which suggests his "white resident" tag really *was* for trolling. He was decidedly not, however, a friend of the LGBT community, as it existed in the 1960s.

Either way... Boaks held the record low for a

candidate in any British parliamentary election - five votes - for over 20 years, until it was broken in 2005.

His campaigning around road safety was ahead of its time, and certainly well-intentioned, even though his methods were perhaps a little over-the-top. He was an advocate of pedestrian and non-motor vehicle traffic rights, and firmly believed that there needed to be more attention and training among road users, emphasising additional care in road safety.

Ironically, Boaks died in a car vs pedestrian crash in 1986, as he was struck by a vehicle while getting off a bus in London. Boaks' funeral was attended by the Minister of Transport, Peter Bottomley. He was buried at sea with full honours in the naval graveyard outside Portsmouth Harbour.

CHARLES E. BOLES (1829-?)

I always prefer to hear about a gentleman rogue than a horrible thug, and Charles "Black Bart" Boles, for all his faults, was both polite and friendly as he robbed his victims blind in the old west.

Born Charles E. Boles in London in 1829, his family emigrated to the still-young United States of America two years later. Boles grew up in New York and in 1849 moved to California, lured by the promise of gold and riches.

Gold and riches weren't really on the cards, unfortunately, as so many prospectors found... and at some point during his years as a prospector he had a run-in with some Wells & Fargo agents - which was not discussed in detail - and vowed revenge against the company. This came to fruition some years later, as Boles adopted the name Black Bart and became one of the most notorious stagecoach robbers ever to operate in California.

As Black Bart, his legend grew due to his leaving poems at his crime scenes, and the fact that (while well-armed) he never fired a shot in anger during his robberies. He was also afraid of horses, so committed all his crimes on foot.[15]

His first stagecoach robbery was on 26 July 1875. He stopped a stagecoach, and demanded the driver hand down his strongbox, calling out to hidden compatriots to shoot the driver if he so much as twitched the wrong way.

The driver, seeing rifle barrels poking out from nearby bushes, complied. It was only after Black Bart had left that he realised that the barrels were fake... just carefully carved wooden poles.

Boles made a little under US$170 from this robbery - which doesn't sound like a great deal, but works out to over US$3500 in today's money.

He was quite prolific and made a few thousand dollars a year from his robberies. Leaving behind some truly terrible poems, and keeping to his apparently strict "no shooting" policy, even when fired upon himself.

I've labored long and hard for bread,
For honor, and for riches,
But on my corns too long you've tread,
You fine-haired sons of bitches.
- Black Bart (1877)[16]

His last stagecoach robbery was on 3 November

1883 and resulted in him being injured. The strongbox was screwed into the base of the coach and took some time to unscrew. During this time, the driver and companion had acquired a rifle, and fired several times as Boles backed out of the stagecoach.

Struck in the hand, Boles had to flee, and - as many criminals seem to do - left behind some incriminating evidence... namely, a laundry token and his glasses... which allowed him to be tracked down by Wells Fargo Detective James B. Hume.

At the time, Boles had been passing himself off as a mining engineer and was living in a modest boarding house in San Francisco.

Arrested, he pleaded guilty, and was sentenced to six years in San Quentin - though he served only four before release. He was described by Police as:

> *A person of great endurance who exhibited genuine wit under most trying circumstances, was extremely proper and polite in behaviour, and eschewed profanity.*

Criminal though he no doubt was, he left an enduring legacy, with annual parades in his honour continuing to this day, and more than one movie, including Black Bart (1948) starring Dan Duryea.

Black Bart was last seen on 28 February 1888 - as Boles headed for the hills and never returned to public life... and though several additional robberies occurred thereafter, with poems left at the scene, the authorities determined that they were copycat crimes, rather than crimes committed by Boles himself.[17]

Johnny Thacker, a Wells Fargo detective who had participated in Boles's arrest, said it was his belief that Boles had emigrated to Japan.[18]

THOMAS BOWDLER (1754-1825)

In New Zealand in the 1980s, a performer by the name of Tina Cross was hired by the government to sing in a public safety advert warning against the dangers of drink-driving.

As she gyrated enticingly on screen - intended to invoke discussion, shock (it was the 80's after all), and so forth - the lyrics to her song included the phrase:

> *Stop making love to the bottle, baby.*
> *You should be making love to me.*

Up with this the prudish elements of New Zealand society absolutely would not put. There was fury, and much writing of scathing letters. Eventually, the Government caved, and the advert was modified. Tina Cross still gyrated enticingly, but now she was singing:

> *Stop making love to the bottle,*

baby. Go and make a cup of tea.

There was a great deal of snortling and chuffawing, as a result. This form of censorship is known as Bowdlerisation. (Or Bowdlerization, if you're American) - It is a form of censorship that involves purging anything deemed noxious or offensive from an artistic work, or other type of writing of media.

From the Enid Blyton stories of old having the names Dick and Fanny being changed to Rick and Frannie (The Faraway Tree), to someone bleeping the f-bomb out of your favourite rap song, to Zeus being a kind family-man in the Disney movies, rather than the vicious womaniser he's made out to be in the original tales... bowdlerisation is everywhere.

It's an odd word... so where did it come from?

Thomas Bowdler. (1754-1825)

Bowdler was an English doctor who found English literature to be just a little bit too much for 19th century sensibilities, and he set about re-writing everything to remove all potential for offence.

He is perhaps best known for publishing The Family Shakespeare, an expurgated edition of William Shakespeare's plays, with all the lewdness and double-entendré removed.[19]

Bowdler's intentions were reasonable enough - and he did at least summarise and justify the changes he had made at the start of each chapter... so perhaps it seems unfair to cast him in too much of a negative light as a result... but should artwork be 'expurgated' to save it from the pearl-clutchers?

> *It's now very common to hear people say, 'I'm rather offended by that.' As if that gives them certain rights. It's actually nothing more... than a whine. 'I find that offensive.' It has no meaning; it has no purpose; it has no reason to be respected as a phrase. 'I am offended by that.' Well, so f**king what.*[20]
> *- Stephen Fry (2005)*

Bowdler's name has become synonymous with expurgation, and his works popularised the practice. He didn't invent it, but he refined it to the point where soon thereafter almost everything that was being released included an expurgated version for the ladies or the children.

We don't need to hide detail from the ladies. And if something is not suitable for children, then they simply shouldn't be exposed to it until they're old enough. I personally don't feel that 'judicious censorship' is the answer.

I can't help but feel that making something more palatable for the masses weakens it. Good books, good art, good movies, and good music should occasionally be uncomfortable. That's what makes them memorable, and what prompts you think.

My take on this is certainly not universal, however. The poet Algernon Swinburne would have *me* cast as a villain:

> *More nauseous and more foolish cant was never chattered than that which would deride the memory or depreciate the merits of Bowdler. No man ever did better service to Shakespeare than the man who made it possible to put him into the hands of intelligent and imaginative children.*

... but then I'm faced with the Disneyfication of folklore... the sweetened porridge of mass-produced literary pap designed to appeal to the widest possible audience... the endless repetition of four-chord songs voiced by spotty teenagers, devoid of spice, and angst, and life... the treasured childhood tales corrupted and sullied because some child's NAME might be considered rude in today's society.[21]

JÓN BRANDSSON, SIGURÐUR ÍSLEIFSSON, AND KETILL KETILSSON

The Great Auk was a seabird endemic to the waters of the North Atlantic. It was once seen in great numbers, but environmental pressure from predators and humans drove it to extinction in the mid-1800s.

It was a bit of an ungainly beast. Walking a bit like a penguin and standing at a fairly diminutive 85cm (33in) tall, it wasn't especially pretty... but it was prized for its feathers, which were particularly shaggy, and fantastic for making pillows.

Firstly, an event known as the Little Ice Age (1400-1800s) resulted in unexpectedly frozen seas, which opened the usual safe nesting sites up to land predators like polar bears.[22] Then hunting by humans began in earnest.

The Great Auk was one of the first animals to have legislation written to protect it. Even in the mid-1500s, protections were laid down to limit where and when the birds could be hunted. This was largely ignored.

By the tail-end of the 1700s, killing the bird for its feathers was outlawed by Britain - though you were still allowed to kill it and use its flesh for bait. In Canada in the late 1700s, you could be publicly whipped for killing a Great Auk.[23] [24]

It was the bird's rarity which drove its downfall. You'd think that would be a given but wait until you hear why. So rare had the animal become, that naturalists[25] were very keen to get their hands on specimens that they could stuff and mount.

When a breeding colony was found off the coast of Iceland in the mid-1830s, they were wiped out almost to a bird by people trying to secure bodies for museums, who would pay a premium. The last two surviving Great Auk were found on the island in 1844, incubating an egg.

Incredibly rare, they were also incredibly

valuable, so two individuals, *Jón Brandsson* and *Sigurður Ísleifsson*, at the request of a merchant, simply walked up to them.

> *They walked slowly. Jón Brandsson crept up with his arms open. The bird that Jón got went into a corner but [mine] was going to the edge of the cliff. It walked like a man ... but moved its feet quickly. [I] caught it close to the edge – a precipice many fathoms deep. Its wings lay close to the sides – not hanging out. I took him by the neck and he flapped his wings. He made no cry. I strangled him. - Sigurður Ísleifsson - interviewed later.*

A third man, *Ketill Ketilsson*, smashed the last remaining Great Auk egg with the heel of his boot.

These three men weren't responsible for the downfall of the species, but they can stand in as proxy for the rest of us for their callous disregard for the last of them.

And thus, the Great Auk was gone forever. Not a particularly noble bird, perhaps, or highly regarded beyond its ability to make bait or pillows... but deserving of a far better fate than it received.

REMARKABLE PEOPLE

When a breeding colony was found off the coast of Iceland in the mid-1830s, they were wiped out almost to a bird by people trying to secure bodies for museums, who would pay a premium.

JOHN ROMULUS BRINKLEY (1885-1942)

If you were a gentleman of a certain age residing in Kansas, and you found that your... um... marital necessity... was lacking in the... er... starch department... then boy, did John Romulus Brinkley have the cure for you.

This one is a bit icky. Be warned.[26]

Unfortunately for the fine, though perhaps not 'upstanding', people who dealt with Brinkley, he was at best a fraud, and at worst a nutter... and his patent cures likely cost the lives of hundreds of people.

For starters, let's be clear... while he certainly promoted himself as a medical genius, he got his diploma through fraudulent means after failing his medical studies. Now, his father had been a medical man, who spent some time as a confederate medic during the American Civil War... so I'd be surprised if Brinkey didn't pick up a trick or two... but he certainly had no formal qualifications.

So, what was it that he did which he said was a cure for not only impotence, but basically all male medical complaints?

Well... you know how there are some restaurants that you go to, and you point at a lobster, and they'll take that lobster and cook it for you? Imagine that, only instead of a lobster it's a goat... and instead of cooking it for you, he would castrate it and surgically insert its testicles into your scrotum. I'll give you a moment to process that.

Brinkley's procedures were totally without scientific merit. The only way they would cause you to ...er... stand to attention ...was because your gentleman sausage was now full of gangrene and was about to drop off.

Dodgy todgers weren't the only claim to villainy Brinkley had, for sure. Refusal to pay child support, kidnapping his own daughter, running up bills and skipping town, openly pro-fascist Nazi sympathiser... he was replete with villainies... but it is his one big quackery which brought him international notoriety.

Obviously, the procedures were only feasible if you're of the approximately 50 percent of the population who has a scrotum... so, for women who were struggling with conceiving, the goat parts were surgically inserted in proximity to the ovaries. I only wish I was joking.

"Surely there wouldn't be anyone stupid enough to have this done to them?!" I hear you cry in disbelief.

Well... he had a 16-room clinic in Kansas, and charged US$750 per operation - just shy of US$10,000 in today's money. They were absolutely not short of business.

Brinkley began promoting goat glands as a cure for 27 ailments, ranging from dementia to emphysema to flatulence. He was absolutely coining it, with the number of customers scuttling out of the woodwork.

He even gave demonstrations, and in full view of the public and press, once transplanted goat testicles into 34 patients, including a judge... who you'd hope would know better.

So... medically, what would happen to you if you'd had goat testicles implanted in your elbow-skin-sporran?

Technically, your body would just absorb them.

Because they were just shoe-horned in to the... sac... without being actually grafted onto anything, rejection usually wouldn't be an issue. It absolutely would not cure you of anything, unless your ailment was a lack of goat testicles.

Lots of people got infections, of course, and several of those died. Brinkey was sued many times for wrongful death over the years... but still he continued. It was such a lucrative procedure.

Lucrative all the way up to the late 1930s, if you can believe it. Eventually the medical community started having conniptions, and Brinkley became the unwilling star of a radio show called "Modern Medical Charlatans", and he was so incensed that made the mistake of suing the broadcaster.

Had he just let it go, he might have weathered the storm... but in bringing about his lawsuit, the onus was on him to prove - in a court of law - that he was not a charlatan, and the moment he took the stand, it became pretty clear that he was an absolute fraud.

The court determined that Brinkley absolutely was a charlatan and a quack. The verdict resulted in dozens of lawsuits, and the Inland Revenue Office started pursuing him for tax fraud. He declared bankruptcy in 1941. He died a year later, penniless and disgraced.

DEACON BRODIE (1741-1788)

Head of the Edinburgh Guild of Cabinetmakers and a fine upstanding member of the community, Brodie was somewhat less salubrious by night... and thought to be one of the inspirations for the tale of Doctor Jekyll and Mr Hyde.

Brodie was born into a fairly wealthy family. His father was Convener of Trades in his hometown of Edinburgh in the mid-1700s. A position of some importance.

This, and a healthy dose of nepotism ensured that Brodie was ranked quite highly among the merchant and trade guilds and earned him a position on the Edinburgh town council.

As a cabinetmaker, Brodie was also a locksmith, and as one of the eminent figures in the town, he rubbed shoulders with the gentry, and became their trusted locksmith and security consultant.

Brodie was the go-to chap for security if you were a lord or lady in Edinburgh at the time... which is unfortunate, because while he was happy being a locksmith by day... he was a burglar by night.

He would make sure that he had copies of keys, and know how to open safes and lockboxes, and would steal from the very people who had employed him to keep their valuables safe.

At one point, in 1768, he stole £800 from a bank for which he had installed locks. That might not seem like a great deal of money, buy when you allow for over two hundred and fifty years of inflation, it works out to £153,560 (US$191,773).

He was earning good money as a legitimate locksmith, earning significantly more as an overnight thief, but spending it as quickly as he was earning it in the flesh markets and gambling dens of 18th century Edinburgh.

Things fell apart in 1788 during a daring armed raid on the excise offices. Believing the place to be empty, Brodie and his three accomplices were singing loudly, rather than creeping through the darkness.[27]

This rather alerted the guard, who it turns out had returned to the offices earlier than expected, and the four-man crew escaped with barely £16 (£3071, or USD$3835).

They would likely have got away clear, had one of

Brodie's accomplices not lost his bottle and gone to the authorities hoping to claim immunity. As a result, all of the accomplices were arrested... though the man did not name Brodie initially at all.

Brodie really put his foot in it, however, by trying to visit the men in prison. He was turned away... but the mistake made Brodie realise that all eyes were now turning towards him, and eyebrows were being raised. He realised that he would have to flee Edinburgh.

Brodie fled initially to London, and then to The Netherlands, where he planned to hide out. He made the mistake of sending letters home, however, and these were intercepted by the authorities, who travelled to The Netherlands and captured the former locksmith, returning him to Edinburgh for trial.

Brodie had made a fool of a lot of very influential people. It was considered very unlikely that any kind of leniency was going to be extended towards him... and indeed, after a remarkably high-profile trial, he was hanged in the High Street, October 1788, in front of a crowd of 40,000 people.

There you might think that the tale would end... and certainly, according to official reports, Brodie was buried in an unmarked grave in the corner of the local cemetery... but there were rumours.

According to the legend... Brodie was hanged while wearing a steel collar, having bribed the hangman, and having arranged for his 'body' to be quickly removed. He was later seen 'at play' in France, presumably in command of quite the fortune.

> *Brodie was rather famously played by Billy Connolly in 1997 in a BBC adaptation of the tale.*

WILLIAM BUCKLAND (1784-1856)

Buckland was an English theologian who became Dean of Westminster. He was also a geologist and palaeontologist. That means he knew a lot about rocks, and dead animals which had since turned into rocks. He was also a loony.

Some of his scientific work was beyond reproach. He was the first person to properly scientifically describe a fossil dinosaur, Megalosaurus, and was able to show prehistoric hyena had lived in a particular cave in Yorkshire.[28]

He was also a zoophage. That is, he would eat basically anything. Took pride in it, in fact.

He claimed he had eaten his way through the entire animal kingdom. He certainly tried to eat at least one of everything during his life and claimed that the worst tasting meals he had ever eaten were bluebottle flies and moles.

This is pretty disgusting, but he would also not balk at eating endangered creatures, which makes him somewhat villainous for starters. He would serve panther, mouse-on-toast, and crocodile to his guests... which I guess is better than feeding his guests to panthers and crocodiles.

Where he really lands squarely on the *WTF DUDE* side of things is when he started eyeing up the religious relics. As well as being a scientist, Buckland was a noted theologian. He had to do a lot of mental wrangling to synchronise his scientific work with his biblical beliefs... but it also gave him an interest in religious matters.

Reportedly, while visiting the church at Nuneham, just outside Oxford, he was made aware of the preserved heart of French king Louis XIV (1643-1715). While being shown it, in the presence of English writer, Augustus Hare, a strange thing happened:

> *"Dr. Buckland, whilst looking at it, exclaimed, 'I have eaten many strange things, but have never eaten the heart of a king before', and, before anyone could hinder him, he had gobbled it up, and the precious relic was lost for ever."*
> *- Augustus Hare*

Buckland died in 1856 at the age of 72, of a neck injury, and his elegy, written some thirty years before his death, read:

> *Where shall we our great Professor inter*
> *That in peace may rest his bones?*
> *If we hew him a rocky sepulchre*
> *He'll rise and break the stones*
> *And examine each stratum that lies around*
> *For he's quite in his element underground.*

PRINCESS CARABOO (? – 1862)

Hailing from the island of Javasu in the Indian Ocean, the unfortunate Princess Caraboo was captured by pirates in the early 1800s. She was taken with them on a long and arduous voyage until she found a means to escape, jumped overboard in the Bristol Channel (England), and swam to shore. The plot of a movie, perhaps? Not at all... read on.

One evening in April of 1817 this young woman (in her early/mid 20s) was found wandering around the coastal village of Almondsbury, Gloucestershire, by a cobbler who realised she was wet, exhausted and disoriented. He took her in, but neither he nor his wife could understand a word she was saying.

They took her to a local magistrate, who determined that the young lady called herself

Caraboo, and spoke a language other than English. After the exhausted Caraboo tried to sleep on the floor, the magistrate took some umbrage.

The natural response, therefore, to finding a young woman who was apparently so down on her luck that she didn't speak the local language, and had not a penny to her name, and apparently nowhere to turn... was to have her locked up in prison for vagrancy.[29]

It was during her imprisonment that she rather fortunately chanced upon a Portuguese sailor, with whom she was able to communicate, and who translated her remarkable tale of woe to officials. Now identified as a foreign princess, Caraboo was subsequently allowed to leave imprisonment. She moved in with the magistrate and his family, as she had nowhere else to stay.

As royalty - albeit from an exotic and faraway land - Princess Caraboo became quite the sensation. She demonstrated an ability to hunt with a bow. She was able to fence. She would swim naked in local waterways - which, let's face it, was always going to draw attention in England in 1817 - and she prayed to a god called she identified as Allah-Talla.

She was subsequently provided with exotic clothing to replace the rags and hand-me-downs with which she had escaped or had been given upon her discovery.

Her exotic nature, and her now rather more exotic look, resulted in a rather famous portrait being painted of her. Local newspapers were entranced, and her story of capture by pirates and subsequent escape became a national wonder. Princess Caraboo shot to near stardom across the length and breadth of England.

This state of affairs lasted for over two months, but stardom - and the quality of the portrait, reproduced in the various newspapers - became her eventual downfall.

You see, a boarding-house keeper in a nearby town recognised the portrait and informed the magistrate and his wife that "Princess Caraboo" was actually none-other than Mary Willcocks, a cobbler's daughter from Witheridge, Devon... around eighty miles away.

Willcocks had been a peripatetic servant in England - but had found herself unemployed and without anywhere to stay. When found by the cobbler on the night she 'had escaped from pirates', she had simply been destitute and lost, saw an opportunity, and invented her fictional language and dreamed up her new character on the spot.

The Portuguese sailor that she had met in prison,

it seems, she had simply charmed so that he supported her tale. A rather fortunate situation for her, as it had provided the independent verification that made her story appear all the more convincing.

Either way, the newspapers of the day went ballistic. They hounded the magistrate and his wife, and used the tale to vilify Willcocks, and promote the concept of a gullible rustic nouveau-middle-class.[30]

Eventually, around a year later, the magistrate and his wife made the incredibly embarrassing and persistent problem of Caraboo go away by paying for Willcocks to travel to America. There she could be free of the stigma of Caraboo, and the hounding of the newspapers... and so would they.

Willcocks moved to Philadelphia, where she lived for a while... but not as Willcocks... as Princess Caraboo. She tried to turn her life story into a stage-show, but notoriety had followed her from England, and the stage show did not do well.

She later returned to England and set herself up in business as a leech farmer, under the pseudonym Mary Burgess, supplying leeches to Bristol Infirmary Hospital... a job she held for the remainder of her life 'in hiding'.

She died from a fall on Christmas Eve 1864, age 72.

REMARKABLE PEOPLE

Local newspapers were entranced, and her story of capture by pirates and subsequent escape became a national wonder. Princess Caraboo shot to near stardom across the length and breadth of England.

CASSIE CHADWICK (1857-1907)

A world-class Canadian fraudster who bankrupted financial institutions and stole a great deal of money during an era when women were not allowed to vote or get loans from the banks.

Born in 1857 in Ontario, she was originally named Elizabeth Bigley. The family was not well off, but was also not destitute. She was known as a liar as a child, and at age 14 opened a bank account using a fraudulent letter and a small amount of cash.

Once she had the account, she passed several worthless cheques to local stores. Being an inexperienced and young fraudster, she was caught very quickly. The courts were lenient due to her age (this was Canada, remember) and she was released without jail time.

A bit of jail time might not have gone amiss, because this was certainly just the start of her life of crime. Three years later, aged 17, Chadwick moved to USA to live with her sister, who had married.

THE STRING OF MEDIUMS AND MARRIAGES

Chadwick did not stay with her sister very long and paid back her hospitality by taking out a loan using the sister's furniture as collateral and moving to Cleveland.

Using this money, she rented an apartment, started calling herself *Madame Lydia DeVere*, and set up shop as a clairvoyant. She operated thus for a while, and while under this pseudonym, married a Doctor Springsteen, who - quite frankly - should have done his due diligence.

I want to say that the Doctor's first name was Bruce, but alas, it was Wallace. It's hard to say how the doctor was fooled, but I suppose we are used to relying on digital records these days. In a world where everything is paper-based, such long-cons must have been rife.

The marriage was photographed, and it was due to this photograph that Chadwick's sister managed to catch up with her and she - and several other 'creditors' - turned up at the Doctor's home and demanded repayment of debts. The doctor - horrified at this point - kicked Chadwick out of the house and sought a divorce, which was granted in 1883. He paid a lot of the debts out of his own pocket.

Down on her luck and now penniless again, Chadwick once more turned to clairvoyancy, only this time she was calling herself Madame Marie LaRose... and she attracted the attention of John Scott the farmer... who she also married.

After four years of farming, she decided she'd had enough, claimed adultery, and filed for divorce. Having fooled him into signing a prenuptial agreement, she took a lot of his money when she left.

Chadwick returned to Cleveland in 1893, changed her name to Cassie Hoover, and... opened a brothel. During this time, she had a son, called Emil.

HUSBAND NUMBER THREE

It made a change from being a clairvoyant, I suppose... but as anyone could have predicted, she met another husband at the place, a Dr Leeroy Chadwick.

Now... you'd think that it was potentially dubious to meet One's husband at a brothel... but again it was a bit of knavery, as the good doctor was there on professional business.[31]

As Cassie had been playing the part of the 'genteel woman' who was running a boarding house, the doctor pointed out that it was, actually, a house of ill-repute. Cassie acted horrified, pretended to faint, and begged the doctor to immediately take her away, before anyone thought she had anything to do with the place.

They married in 1897. Chadwick had not told the doctor that she had a son, or that the child was in the care of one of the women at the brothel. Certainly, during a court case for forgery shortly afterwards (that she had managed to keep from the doctor), she identified herself as a single woman (Cassie Chadwick) with no children.

Chadwick had landed on her feet, for the good doctor was extremely wealthy, and ran in the finest social circles.

HIGH SOCIETY AND THE CARNEGIE CON

Unfortunately, Chadwick was something of a social pariah. Her tendency to try to buy favour made the wealthy withdraw from her, and she was certainly not well-loved. She was invited to events only because of the social standing of her husband.

Chadwick began spending up large, running up many debts, before turning her hand fully to forgery and the con to end all cons. The plan was relatively complex and involved inveigling herself into the affairs of the extremely wealthy Carnegie family in New York.

Chadwick convinced her husband's lawyer to accompany her to the Carnegie residence. She went inside and spoke to the housekeeper, and upon returning, 'accidentally' dropped a forged promissory note for $2 million with the signature of Carnegie himself! That's roughly $50 million in today's money.

The lawyer picked it up and returned it to her, but not before reading it, and the bait had been taken. He was fooled. He now believed that she was the illegitimate daughter of Andrew Carnegie, one of the wealthiest men in America, and that Carnegie was paying her off.

After she claimed that Carnegie had been doing this for a while, and that she had $7 million in other notes, and was set to inherit $400 million upon Carnegie's death, the lawyer set her up with a safety deposit box and a promise of utmost discretion.

... which he broke almost immediately.

Upon hearing that Chadwick was the heir to the Carnegie fortune, banks and other institutions across North America and Canada started offering her services and lines of credit at horrendous interest rates.

The bankers all assumed that Carnegie would vouch for any debts and that they would be fully repaid anyway once Carnegie died. They declined to check further, because nobody wanted to embarrass Carnegie or reveal that they knew his 'dirty little secret'.

One person, however, who had loaned Chadwick almost $200,000 became concerned when he heard about all the other loans that Chadwick had accumulated. Indeed, she had purchased diamond necklaces, enough clothes to fill 30 closets, and a gold organ of all things.[32]

This creditor - Herbert B. Newton from Massachusetts - demanded repayment of the debt, and when repayment was not forthcoming, approached Carnegie directly. Carnegie, of course, denied ever knowing Chadwick, and grumbled that he had not signed a promissory note in more than three decades.

So, it all began to fall apart, as of course it was always going to. Creditors demanded money, and there was no money. Individuals sued; organisations sued. Charges were laid. Chadwick was arrested while trying to flee Cleveland and was found with a money-belt containing $100,000 on her.

Doctor Leeroy Chadwick filed for divorce immediately and fled with the rest of his family to Europe.[33]

The news of Chadwick's arrest sent the Cleveland banking community into uncontrolled spasms.

One bank, which had loaned her close to a million dollars suffered a massive run that forced it into bankruptcy.

This was at the time the biggest financial crime in US history, and one which became front-page news around the world. On 10 March 1905 a Cleveland court sentenced Chadwick to 14 years in prison. Chadwick never saw freedom again and died - likely of a stroke - in Columbus penitentiary 10 October 1907.

KING CHARLES VI (1380-1422)

It's hard to be a king, I'm sure. All that lording it over people must really be a strain. Especially back in the day when the power of a king was practically absolute, and you could pretty-much do whatever you wanted. Mix this with a smidgeon of lunacy, and what you have is Charles VI in the late 1300s.

It actually all seemed to be going well for King Charles VI of France when he first came to power. He came to the throne very young and didn't actually get to do much more than act as a figurehead until he reached his 20s.

He was, however, both able and popular, and about as normal is it was possible to be in the monarchy in the 14th century.

There was the usual amount of hunting and the requisite amount of wine, women, and amateur dramatics that goes on in a young man's life[34]

- especially if they're not too worried where the next meal is coming from and have a bit of money to chuck about.

It's probably much easier to gad about drinking and wenching if you're a king. It's not like you need to hold down a proper job or keep your grades up, and there's a whole palace full of people ready to clean up after you. Carousing is almost part of the job description.

Also, there's the whole French aspect. When it came to the 'wine' part of the equation, they've had the edge for a very long time. A Frenchman knows how to throw a party.

It was therefore somewhat of a surprise when during a particularly normal hunt while on campaign in the forest of Le Mans in 1392, Charles had some kind of fit, flew into an unstoppable rage, and cold-bloodedly murdered four of his retinue.

The reason isn't known. It could have just been a psychotic break of some description, but there is supposition that he was poisoned (either accidentally or by design) and it affected him in an unanticipated way.

You'd think he'd have got into trouble for that but... well, being a King then was not like it would be now. You can't just knock someone's block off in today's society if you're European royalty. It doesn't fly.

I'm not one to mock someone for mental illness. There's enough of it about even in the modern world, it's stupidly taboo to talk about, and there's no way in hell that it would have been properly diagnosed back in the day - even if there was a treatment available.[35]

The rest of his reign was also somewhat unusual. Charles became convinced that he was made of glass and would shatter at a moment's notice... which seems at odds with his tendency to run naked through the palace screaming that he was Saint George, or covering himself with pitch (along with friends) and gate-crashing weddings dressed as 'wild-men' to engage in rowdy, bawdy - and likely wedding-ruining - nonsense.

The latter being rather unfortunate, because due to an accident with a naked flame, several of his pitch-coated companions caught fire in what came to be known as the 'ball of the burning men'.

I mean, what the actual hell? I don't know if you've ever mucked about with pitch, but it's not the sort of thing you want to get on you, let alone COVER yourself in. The damn stuff just doesn't come off, and even leaving aside the horrific flammability, there's something fundamentally undignified about sticking to literally everything.[36]

Charles was in power when England's Henry V decided that France had to give some of its real-estate back, and the famous Battle of Agincourt occurred on his watch.

A capable king, at this point, may have been able to aid the French forces in driving off the English invaders, but Charles was in no fit state to do much more than gibber and swing from the rafters.[37]

Oh, there were lots of notable events in Charles' reign, such as the ongoing wars with Burgundy and England, the expulsion of the Jews in 1394, the struggles for power in the court as a result of his inconsistency, and his refusal to bathe or change his clothes for five months... but eventually it all came to an end in 1422, when he died.[38]

What followed was a period of instability in France[39], which included the arrival of *Joan of Arc* (1429) and the restoration of the French line with Charles VII - The Victorious.

JOHN MALCOLM THORPE FLEMING CHURCHILL (1906-1996)

Churchill was a British Army officer who fought in the Second World War with a longbow, bagpipes, and a Scottish broadsword.

This is, if nothing else, suitable grounds for declaring someone 'remarkable'. Even a little odd, if pushed, though I'm sure half of my readers go through life with a longbow and a set of bagpipes at the ready... but Churchill led a very interesting life.

PRE-WAR

Born in Ceylon, which is now Sri Lanka, Churchill's father was an engineer of some repute, who's job took him all over the British

Empire... for indeed, 'twas an empire back in the day. The family settled in England shortly before the end of the first world war, when Churchill was a tweenager.

This didn't stop him travelling, however. In the between-war years, he moved briefly to Nairobi, where he worked as both a newspaper editor, and a male model. He had a small role in several movies, and won some awards for bagpiping, and archery.[40]

Then World War II broke out, and things got decidedly weird.

1940

Joining the British Expeditionary Force to stop the German invasion of France, he and his men ambushed a German patrol. Churchill is said to have given the signal to attack by raising his claymore broadsword, and it is even rumoured that he used a bow and arrow to dispatch a German soldier.

He became famous for his absolute belief that a military officer who was not equipped with a sword was not properly dressed. He also acquired the nicknames "Fighting Jack Churchill", and "Mad Jack"... for taking a broadsword, bow and arrows, and bagpipes with him everywhere.

After fighting in Dunkirk, Churchill joined the Commandos, and things got even weirder.

1941

During a raid on a garrison in Vågsøy, Norway, he exited the landing craft playing bagpipes, before throwing a grenade and charging headlong into battle. He was awarded the Military Cross and Bar after the action.

1943

Two years later, in Italy, his Commando unit was tasked with capturing a German observation post. With only one man for help, he infiltrated the town in which the observation post was located, and captured 42 enemy soldiers, holding them at bow-and-arrow point.

While in hand-to-hand combat, he lost his broadsword, so after returning the captured soldiers to his command, he turned around and trudged back into the enemy-held town to retrieve it.

On the way there, he met some US soldiers heading in the wrong direction and is said to have warned them that he would not come and rescue them if they didn't turn around, as "he'd be damned if he was going to walk up this road for a third time".

1944

The following year, his Commando unit was in Yugoslavia. Things did not go well. He was tasked with raiding the island of Brač, which was under

German control.

The landing went well, but when Churchill was accidentally strafed by an RAF Spitfire, and the partisan troops failed to support his commando team, he was left by himself playing the bagpipes in the face of an overwhelming German advance.

They captured him, and - incorrectly thinking he was related to Winston Churchill - took him to Berlin for interrogation, before later sending him to a concentration camp in Oranieburg with other 'prominent' prisoners.

Churchill escaped, was captured after travelling most of the way to the Baltic coast on foot.

1945

The tail-end of World War II saw Churchill transferred to a camp overseen by SS troops. With the war going badly, the SS troops appear to have been preparing to murder their prisoners in cold-blood, and it was likely that it was only the intervention by regular German troops that saved Churchill's life.[41]

Churchill and the other prisoners were simply released to fend for themselves. So, he walked over 90 miles south to Italy, where he met up with an American armoured column, and was ultimately repatriated.

Victory in Europe saw Churchill being shipped to Burma, where the war was still running hot.

However, by the time he arrived, the US forces had dropped two nuclear bombs on Japan, and the war ended.

This did not meet with Churchill's somewhat bloodthirsty approval, and he is famously referenced as saying:

> *"If it wasn't for those damn Yanks, we could have kept the war going another 10 years!"*

POST WAR

The end of the war did not see the end of combat for Churchill. He was involved with the evacuation of Jewish civilians from Jerusalem after a massacre of medical workers by Arab forces, before retiring from combat in 1948.

He then had a bit part in the classic movie Ivanhoe (1952) where he played an archer shooting from atop Warwick Castle.

During a brief sojourn to Australia, where he helped train future soldiers, he became absolutely hooked on surfing, and upon his return to Britain, was the first person to surf the River Severn man-high tidal-bore in Wales.

He died in 1996, just a few months shy of his 90th birthday.

JEANNE DE CLISSON (1300-1359)

Born in Western France, on the Atlantic Coast, Jeanne de Clisson was the daughter of a nobleman. She inherited land and title upon his untimely death. She grew up to become a fierce and terrible opponent to the tyranny of the French monarchy.

A String of Marriages

Her first marriage was in 1312 to a 19-year-old Breton nobleman, who was already a widower.

Yeah, she was twelve and he was 19. That's not the sort of thing that would fly in today's society, but such things were relatively commonplace in the 1300s, particularly when marriages were also a tool to cement alliances between noble families. She had her first child at age 14, and a second at age 16.

It should be pointed out, I suppose, that the average life expectancy for someone living in western Europe at around this time was somewhere around age 24. You had to start young, because chances are you were going to end young. This has improved considerably, of course, with the average life expectancy in the same region now hovering at around 82 years.

Alas, her husband died in 1326, and two years later, Jeanne re-married - this time to a nobleman 13 years her senior - ostensibly to provide protection for her young children. He was the son of the duke of the Duke of Brittany, so quite well off.

At first things seemed to be going quite well, but there came an opportunity for the Ducal family to make a much better match than poor Jeanne, so she was cast aside - marriage annulled - after some courtly intrigue, so that her (former) husband could now marry the niece of Phillip VI of France.

This did not go down well at all. Fortunately, as the marriage was annulled, the son of the Duke was not permitted to keep her lands - which he was entitled to as her husband. The whole thing got pointedly papal at one point.

In 1330, she married for the third time, to Olivier IV de Clisson, a remarkably wealthy Breton

Marche Lord and Knight in the court of Phillip VI. The marriage finally seemed to be one in which Jeanne could be happy and was even perhaps of her choosing. Along with her own lands, their combined wealth was impressive, and likely drew jealous eyes from rivals in the court.[42]

Unfortunately, Olivier IV became embroiled in palace intrigue, and after an untimely military defeat in defence of his King's lands was accused of treason, without much evidence.

After being tortured to secure a confession, he was hung, drawn, and quartered, with his head displayed on a pike in the coastal city of Nantes.[43]

The Black Fleet

Jeanne was absolutely furious, as you can imagine, and declared her intent to end the line of Phillip VI. She sold absolutely every asset she had, raised an army of around 400 men, and started attacking French assets in Brittany.

One of the exciting things about Europe in the 1300s was that there was no shortage of folk who were willing to take up arms and loyally support your noble cause... right up until the money ran out. There was probably never a better time to be a mercenary.

Jeanne and her army stormed the castle at Touffou and massacred everyone inside bar one individual to spread the word. They then wiped out a garrison not far from Nantes.

With the money left over, the extra cash raised in her raids, and with the help of Breton nobles who were anti-France, as well as assistance from England, Jeanne purchased three warships, and had them painted black, and equipped for harassing French shipping.

They were The Black Fleet, and her flagship was called My Revenge.[44]

They hunted French ships in the Bay of Biscay and the English Channel, wiping out entire crews, with the exception of one or two to spread the tale of Jeanne's revenge.

Captured ships were added to her fleet.

It was mainly commerce raiding against lightly armed targets, and in lieu of cannon, the targeted ships were grappled and boarded, with much of the combat occurring on deck with crossbows and swords.

The Black Fleet also raided up and down the Normandy coast, putting villages to the flame.

While Jeanne was not technically speaking working for the English (there is no evidence of a letter of marque to allow privateering activity) she did supply English forces when they raided into French territory.

The My Revenge was eventually sunk by French ships, after a pitched battle, leaving Jeanne adrift for five days, and resulting in the death of one of her children, but after her eventual rescue, her piracy against the French continued for over a decade.

She became known as The Lioness of Brittany and her actions almost certainly hurt Phillip VI considerably. He eventually died a broken man not long after Jeanne's 50th birthday.

The Fourth Marriage

Once the man responsible for the murder of her third husband is no more, Jeanne settles down and marries again - this time to Gautier Bentley, one of King Edward III's military deputies.

Together they reclaimed Jeanne's castles and land from the French... though King Edward III demanded that they be handed back due to treaty arrangements. The pair refused, and Bentley was briefly held in custody in the Tower of London until his plea to retain the land and castles was heard.

The heavy fighting between France and England had all but petered out, mainly due to the depredations of the Black Plague, which had wiped out a fifth of the European population at this stage... so Bentley was basically just let go.

They still had to relinquish the land, but in 1357

Walter and Jeanne were granted the barony of La Roche-Moisan as compensation. They lived on their new lands, with their allies, on the Atlantic coast for two years until they both died within weeks of each other, Jeanne age 59.

Jeanne was absolutely furious, as you can imagine, and declared her intent to end the line of Phillip VI. She sold absolutely every asset she had, raised an army of around 400 men, and started attacking French assets in Brittany.

ROBERT COATES (1772-1848)

Robert "Romeo" Coates was an English eccentric, best remembered for his career as an amateur actor. His self-image included a highly mistaken belief in his own thespian prowess.

Coates was a wealthy man, having inherited a sugar plantation in the west indies, and a large collection of diamonds. He used this to fund his acting 'habit', much to the detriment of those who lived near him in his hometown of Bath, United Kingdom.

He loved his Shakespeare, and from the early 1800s onwards would appear in plays like Romeo and Juliet, and he would always play the male lead. He would often make up scenes and dialog on the fly and would frequently repeat parts that he liked... usually dramatic death scenes... three or four times in one single play.

He claimed he was the best actor in Britain... but people were largely turning up to see if he was really as bad as everyone was saying... and by all accounts he genuinely was.

He would also put himself in charge of costuming, though he seemed to not really have the knack. Here is a note regarding his costume design for Romeo:

> *"It had a flowing, sky-blue cloak with sequins, red pantaloons, a vest of white muslin, a large cravat, and a plumed "opera hat," not to mention dozens of diamonds. The too-small garments caused him to move stiffly, and at some point, the seat of his pants split open. The audience roared with laughter."*
> *- Captain Rees Howell Gronow*

His antics on-stage included a 20-minute search for a dropped diamond buckle, offering to share snuff with audience members in the vaunted 'box' seats, and dusting the stage with a handkerchief before 'dying' on it.

Then, faced with shouts of "Die again, Romeo!", he acted out Romeo's death twice - and was about to attempt a third before his Juliet came back to life and shouted at him.

I genuinely begin to wonder if he was honestly a terrible actor, or a comic genius, two hundred years ahead of his time. I hope this is true, but I suspect the truth of the matter is that he was simply delusional, and thought he was *the business*.

For a while, he was extremely popular... but around 1816, people were becoming tired of this famously bad actor, and his audiences began to dwindle. You have to give credit to Coates, however. He never tried to make money from his acting and his plays. They were all put on for charity, and he supported many a worthy cause... making him a remarkable person.

Robert Coates died in London in 1848 after a street accident. He was caught and crushed between a Hansom cab and a private carriage as he was leaving a performance at the Theatre Royal, Drury Lane.

WILLIAM COLEPAUGH (1918-2005)

One of the last two German spies believed to be operating in the United States during World War II, William Colepaugh was less about the mission, and more about the ladies.

Colepaugh's story starts in the early 1940s. He was a Navy man, and part of the US Navy Reserve. For less than a year. He was honourably discharged, though official paperwork stated the discharge was "for the good of the Navy", suggesting some undisclosed shenanigans.

This apparently did not sit well with Colepaugh, who - knowing the sea and little else - returned to service in the merchant marine as a lowly mess boy. He apparently did not enjoy this much either, so after a few months he jumped ship in Lisbon and made haste to the German Consulate to defect.

Clearly, it was wartime, and this was treason of the highest order, and hanging was still a punishment for such activity. Still, the Germans decided there was potentially some merit in having an American in their pocket, so after extensive training in espionage techniques, and buddied with a well-trained German officer, Erich Gimpel, the young Colepaugh became a spy. Returned to mainland America by U-boat in 1944, his mission began.

The mission (Operation Magpie) was to gather technical information regarding the Allied war effort and transmit it back to Germany using a radio the two men were expected to build. To help them, they were sent ashore with a small fortune (around US$700,000 in today's money) in cash and diamonds.

Colepaugh was not at all happy with this. He wanted to be part of the powerful German army - not sneaking around like some kind of louse in America's undergarments. He was not given much option, however.

As the U-boat (U-1230) had unfortunately sunk some allied shipping in US waters, the powers-that-be knew there was a good chance that there were some spies ashore, and made it public that any unusual persons doing unusual things should be reported to the authorities.

The two spies at this point had travelled by train to New York. They were to inveigle themselves into positions where they could observe and report on the war effort. When met with a general air of paranoia from a city on the edge, Colepaugh decided that the best way to complete his mission was...

... well, he took all the money that the spies had brought, and blew it on wine, women, and song. Partying it up in New York like it was 1999 and not 1944. Colepaugh might not have had James Bond's instincts for espionage, but he did share Bond's fondness for alcohol, and the ladies... and the ladies either liked him, or his pockets full of money and diamonds.

For a whole month, he partied and caroused with local women, got ruinously drunk, completely forgetting about the mission. He was apparently insatiable... really putting the 'aroused' into 'caroused'.

Then, afraid of Gimpel, and perhaps experiencing burnout, or possibly thinking he might have been a little *too* obviously out of the ordinary, he handed himself in to the FBI and told them everything. This included handing over Gimpel, hoping to secure immunity against prosecution, or leniency at the very least. He failed at both.

The Attorney General immediately handed both

men over to the US Military, all but ensuring they were sentenced to be executed.

Gimpel was sentenced to death by firing squad. Colepaugh was sentenced to death by hanging. It seems that the US Military might have been happy that Colepaugh had handed himself and Gimpel in, but it was clear that they were generally not disposed to be nice to him.

Fortunately for the two men, President Truman was sworn in only a few days before they were due to be executed. He was a long-time opponent to capital punishment, and with Germany on the cusp of surrender, he commuted their death sentences to life imprisonment.

The loyal spy, Gimpel, was finally released from prison in 1955 and returned to Germany, where he wrote a best-selling book of his experiences. Colepaugh - who had blown the operation and handed the whole lot to the authorities - didn't get out for another five years, in 1960. They really didn't like him, it seems.

The remainder of Colepaugh's post-prison life was as a business owner, selling lockers, desks and other metal office products. A pedestrian end to a somewhat brief and unusual, but certainly remarkable, military 'career'.

He further declined to speak about his experiences or motivations, and ultimately volunteered with the Boy Scouts and became a member of Rotary. Colepaugh died in 2005 from complications due to Alzheimer's.

JACKIE COOGAN (1914-1984)

John Leslie "Jackie" Coogan was an American actor and comedian who began his film career as a child actor in silent films, working alongside such actors as Charlie Chaplin.

Born in 1914, Coogan's life was looking rosy. His first role was as an infant in 1917's Skinner's Baby. He was discovered by the incredibly famous Charlie Chaplin while on stage, and his career took off. He starred in a considerable number of movies, as well as some absolute classics, such as The Kid (1921), and Oliver Twist (1922).

He was also one of the first Hollywood stars to be merchandised, and a great deal of money was to be made on Jackie Coogan themed peanut butter, stationery, whistles, dolls, records, coins, and figurines, among other stuff.

Throughout his childhood, Coogan earned somewhere in the region of $4 million, which works out to around $58 million in today's money. Jackie's money was managed by this father, John Henry Coogan Jr right up until John's death in May 1935 in a car accident. Jackie was the sole-survivor in this crash, which took the lives of his father, his best friend, and several others.

When Jackie turned 21 in October that same year, he sought to claim his money. Unfortunately, his mother had married a financial advisor by the name of Arthur Bernstein, and between them, they had squandered almost the entire fortune... spending the sum on fur coats, diamonds, expensive cars, and property.

Jackie Coogan found that he was 21 and practically penniless. While he was still acting, he was, at this point, certainly not a high-earning child star like he was back in his early years. His mother claimed that Jackie, as a child, thought he was playing in front of the camera, and that anything earned by a child before the age of 21 belonged to the parents.

> *Mr. and Mrs. Bernstein will never be serious contenders for the title of Mr. and Mrs. America.*
> *- New York Herald Tribune, 1938*
>
> *No promises were ever made to give Jackie anything.*
> *- Lillian Rita Coogan/Bernstein, 1938*

He sued his mother and stepfather in 1938,

trying to recover some of his earnings. After legal fees, he recovered a grand total of $126,000... which let's face it was still quite a lot of money for the age, even if it wasn't $4 million.

I can understand the parents - step or otherwise - feeling it would be reasonable to take an income from Jackie's earnings. I would even not bat too much of an eyelid if they'd decided to take 50 percent... but beyond a certain limit I personally feel that it becomes morally bankrupt, regardless of what the law might allow.

Jackie was so poor during litigation that his friend Charlie Chaplin gave him $1,000 for legal expenses without even a second thought... or chances are he'd have got nothing.

As a result of the ruling, and the extreme publicity it engendered, the following year California enacted a bill which protected child stars and their income to some extent, and it was known as Coogan's Law, or The Coogan Act.

Coogan went on to become a glider pilot in World War II and flew allied troops behind enemy lines into the Burmese jungle. After the war his acting career took off again, and many will remember his role as Uncle Fester in the 1960s original Addams Family series.

Jackie Coogan died in 1984 from a heart attack, aged 69. His legacy being some truly memorable roles, hazardous duty in World War II, a handful of successful children, and a bill to protect those child actors to come after him from unscrupulous parents.

SALVADOR DALI (1904-1989)

Dali was born in 1904 in Catalonia, Spain, to a middle-class family. His father was a strict disciplinarian, though his mother very-much encouraged his art from a young age.

Dali was anything but typical growing up. To start with, his parents told him he was the reincarnation of his brother, aged three when he died to a vicious stomach bug, nine months before Dali was born. That's bound to do a number on your noodle.

Throughout the remainder of his life, his dead brother would be referenced in his writing and his artwork, so it was clearly something that stuck with him.

TROUBLED ADOLESCENCE
Dali had something of a masochistic streak, and was notorious for hurting himself on purpose, later writing "the pain was insignificant, the

pleasure immense" - which he briefly attempted to share with friends, as he pushed one of his peers off a low bridge. The child had minor injuries and lay there calling for help while Dali apparently calmly sat eating cherries.

His schooling suffered, and he was expelled twice - once for starting a riot, though the details are scarce - and the second time for shouting down professors during an exam, which he subsequently refused to take, citing that he was far more intelligent than they.

OBSESSION WITH TYRANNY

Let's also add his self-professed sexual dreams about Hitler into the mix.[45] Dali stated outright that the dictator's rise to power affected him in the 'most intimate' ways. He even went so far as to paint erotic scenes of the tyrant.

It wasn't just the German Chancellor that held sway in Dali's mind. He was quite friendly with the fascist Spanish ruler Francisco Franco, even though the artist kept talking about how he was entirely apolitical.

The FBI kept records on Dali largely because they were fairly convinced that he was a Nazi sympathiser.

Dali was actually confronted by his local artistic community about the issue, and he tried to excuse his actions and statements by saying that he wasn't a fascist... just a pervert.

> *I often dreamed of Hitler as a woman. His flesh, which I had imagined whiter than white, ravished me...*
> *- Salvador Dali, 1934*

The famous author George Orwell wrote of Dali at the time, staying that he was "a disgusting human being" with "undeniably exceptional gifts".

LATER WEIRDNESS

Dali was a surrealist, of course, and he applied this to his personal life. He would drive around in a Rolls Royce handing out cauliflowers, by the dozen, to people randomly on the street, claiming to be fascinated by their "logarithmic curve".

Honestly, I started this section with the intent to list a few of the eccentricities - particularly in Dali's later life - but there are far too many to list in great detail.

He had a pet ocelot.[46] He once suggested Cher masturbate with a toy fish. He killed a bat with his teeth so he could watch it being eaten by ants. At one point he decided to stop eating in order to go into hibernation like some bacteria he had read about.

... and all of this is before you factor in his art, which touched on many styles, but hovered inexorably around surrealism. From melting clocks, to people eating each other, and self-described with phrases like "a vast human body breaking out into monstrous excrescences of arms and legs tearing at one another in a delirium of auto-strangulation".

Still, if being weird was illegal, everyone would get arrested sooner or later... though Dali would be a hard act to follow. He was certainly an unusual and remarkable fellow, who left behind a significant and influential legacy of artwork. Dali died in 1988 of heart failure, and was buried in his own museum in Figueres, Spain.

FRANCIS DASHWOOD (1708-1781)

He's not the Messiah... he's a very naughty boy!
- Monty Python's Life of Brian

With many try-hard villainous types, it is hard to take them seriously, as they strut and preen and flounce their way through life, casting petty unpleasantness about them like an angry toddler with a handful of turds.

Francis Dashwood, a Londoner, on the other hand, had a jolly good go at being quite the rotter.

One of his first claims to fame was his attempts to impersonate King Charles XII of Sweden while on a tour of Russia, during which time he tried to seduce the Tsarina - a feat which got him expelled from the region in some disgrace.[47]

Now, if you were wealthy (and Dashwood was

excessively wealthy) the in thing was to have your own Dining Club. That is, basically, a group of your bestest mates who would all come around once a month and cause havoc with you.

Many of you will have your own posse. Imagine that, only with powdered wigs, considerably more roast ox, strict rules about which way to pass the alcohol, and no WiFi... and you're probably getting there.

Dashwood started with The Dilettanti Society, which was a periodic drunken set-to, but ultimately a fairly tame affair, and described as:

> *A club for which the nominal qualification is having been to Italy, and the real one, being drunk; the two chiefs are Lord Middlesex and Sir Francis Dashwood, who were seldom sober the whole time they were in Italy.*
> *- Horace Walpole (1743)*

So, not really the vehicle for villainy that you might think, under the circumstances, but certainly a herald for things yet to pass. Dashwood became a Member of Parliament, and it should be mentioned that he did try to encourage public works to reduce unemployment... though this failed.

That doesn't sound villainous though, does it? Weeeeell... the public works in question were to expand the Hellfire Caves, in which Dashwood had a vested interest... so he was really trying to use public money, and co-opt unemployed people, to suit his own agenda.

Then there's *The Hellfire Club*.

Dashwood's wealth and power enabled him to rent and rebuild the derelict *Medmenham Abbey* along the banks of the Thames River, and therein he - now in his late 40s - and several of his cronies installed The Hellfire Club - in approximately 1755.

Dashwood, certainly no prude, presided over the club dressed as a monk (Saint Francis of Assisi, as it happens). The building itself bore the motto "Fais ce que tu voudrais", which translates from the French as "Do whatever you want"... and they certainly did.

As the gossip goes, he and his posse would hire prostitutes, dress them as nuns, and have drunken orgies which parodied religious rites. Even those who could be described as "of a more liberal persuasion" would shrink from outlining the goings-on when the club was in session.

Having said that, gossip was a growth industry back in the mid-1700s, so in reality the wicked rumours of the Hellfire Club are far more likely to have just focused on cards, backgammon, and... well... some libertinage for sure... mistresses and what not.

Later in his life, Dashwood's influence enabled him to adopt the role of Chancellor of the Exchequer (a senior minister and head of Her Majesty's Treasury), but while this came with great power - he had absolutely no clue what he was doing and had been promoted well over his head.

> *"Of financial knowledge he did not possess the rudiments, and his ignorance was all the more conspicuous from the great financial ability of his predecessor. His budget speech was so confused and incapable that it was received with shouts of laughter."*
> *- Pollard 1901, p. 114 cites Lecky, History, ed. 1892, iii. 224.*

He subsequently retired into relative obscurity and died at West Wycombe after a long illness in 1781.

PIERRE DE LANCRE (1553-1631)

Every now and again, reading about villains throws up a nasty piece of work, and de Lancre certainly qualifies. He was a witch-hunter in France, and his sadistic zeal saw dozens of people - mostly women - executed for witchcraft in the 16th and 17th centuries.

The first thing I suppose that I should get out of the way is that back in the 16th and 17th centuries, people really did believe in witches. Not in a cynical "I might get my neighbour's land if I accuse them of witchcraft" kind of way (though that certainly happened), but in a very real, very frightened kind of way.

Back then, bad things didn't just happen. Things made them happen. If your goat died under mysterious circumstances, nobody knew about Parisian Goat Flu, or Epigoatitis, or Hooflingtons Perriwobbles of the Feta Pouch... they just assumed that the little old lady who walked past and gave it a bit of carrot because she likes goats was a witch who killed it on purpose.

Next thing you know, there's a trial, or a mob, and poor old Nanny Dawkins from down the road, who just happens to like goats[48], and had a spare bit of carrot, is being tied to a ducking stool[49] and is going 'splish' down the local pond.

Today we can look back on it and say it's ignorant, and cruel, and unnecessary, but people believed it, and because people are - by and large - quite happy to be awful to each other... well.

Throw into this the power of organised religion at the time, and their willingness to stir things into a frenzy for a variety of reasons (not the least among them being 'divide and conquer') and you have an era rife with serious men in serious hats trying to encourage you to set fire to your grandma.

Born into this rather chaotic period of history, we have Pierre de Lancre. An educated and highly religious man, he became a judge in Bordeaux, southern France, from the age of 29, and was instructed shortly thereafter by King Henry IV to stamp out the scourge of witchcraft in the province of Labourd.[50]

His family was of Basque stock - something they took great pains to dissociate themselves from, as the Basque people were seen to be ignorant and superstitious (irony in itself) - but this seemed to have fostered a rather strong hatred of Basques in de Lancre's life.

So... when de Lancre started finding witches in 1609, at the birth of what became known as the Witch Hunt of Labourd, it is no surprise that no small number of them were of Basque origin.

The judge had around seventy people executed by fire in the course of a single year - burned at the stake - and he was on a roll. He estimated that there were some 3,000 witches still at large in Labourd alone, and that they needed to be winkled out with great diligence.

There were only around 30,000 people living in Labourd at the time, so this kind of fanaticism was clearly not seen as healthy by anyone - including, as it happens, the people who set de Lancre on this course in the first place... so he was dismissed from office shortly thereafter.

The tide of popular opinion was shifting somewhat, in light of de Lancre's excesses. Certainly, from this point on in Bordeaux, cases of witchcraft tended to be treated very leniently, with plenty of room for appeal - almost apologetically.

That didn't really stop de Lancre from railing against witchcraft - though the body-count had reduced considerably. He took instead to writing books, in a desperate attempt to convince people that witches weren't just some imagined problem - but a very real existential threat.

Many of the official records of this period of history were lost due to later revolutions, but de Lancre's books survived, and these detailed his methods and his rationale.

> *"To dance indecently; eat excessively; make love diabolically; commit atrocious acts of sodomy; blaspheme scandalously; avenge themselves insidiously; run after all horrible, dirty, and crudely unnatural desires; [snip] —are these not the uncontrolled characteristics of an unparalleled lightness of being and of an execrable inconstancy that can be expiated only through the divine fire that justice placed in Hell?"*
> *- Pierre de Lancre*
>   *Tableau de l'Inconstance des Mauvais Anges et Demons (1612)*

His books also mark him as a dreadful misogynist, antisemite, and virulent in his hatred of... well, apparently just about everything.

Through his actions, de Lancre has been described by many writers throughout the years as bigoted, due to his stance against those of Basque heritage, as well as infantile, gloating, sadistic, and gleeful in response to how he acted during trials and executions.

It is not clear how much of this is accurate, but given the clear vehemence de Lancre felt towards what he saw as a deluge of witchcraft in rural France, it would not surprise many if he took great pleasure in enacting his duties as witch-hunter.

What impact he personally had on witch hunting in general is somewhat up for debate. His actions in Labourd almost certainly prompted the Basque witch trials just south of the French border, in which the Spanish Inquisition (who expected them?!) tried over 7,000 cases of witchcraft... and he likely influenced plenty of others.

HORACE DE VERE COLE (1881-1936)

William Horace de Vere Cole was an eccentric prankster born in Ballincollig, County Cork, Ireland.

It takes a special kind of someone to be historically labelled "a prankster". These are, generally speaking, not the sort of person you'd want to sit next to at a formal dinner or, quite honestly, generally associate with at all.[51]

Cole appears to have been an exception.

His remarkable life covers both the mundane and the extraordinary. The extreme ends of the scale for example were to (a) pretend to be the uncle of the Sultan of Zanzibar to be ceremonially received by Cambridge University, and (b) to walk down a London high-street with a cow udder poking out of his pants. When he found he had accumulated enough outraged followers, he would cut it off with a pair of scissors.

He once challenged a local MP to a foot race on a London street, giving him a 10 yard head-start. He had already slipped his gold watch into the MP's pocket, and when they ran past a police-officer, he shouted "STOP! THIEF!", and the MP was arrested for theft. After owning up to the gag, Cole himself was arrested, and fined £5 for breach of the peace.

He once hosted a party, and upon talking to one another, all the attendees found out that they had the word 'bottom' as part of their surnames. Now, I'm not sure if that counts as a prank, but it's definitely a niche gag which only a few would likely appreciate.

Probably my favourite gag, however, was his attendance at a West End play. He felt the play was horribly pretentious and detested it. So, he purchased eight seats in the middle of the front row, and employed eight bald (but hat-wearing) men to sit in them. As the show started, they would take off their hats, and on top of their heads, he'd had a single letter painted, so that together they spelled "B-O-L-L-O-C-K-S".[52]

His most famous prank, however, was that upon the captain of the flagship of the Royal Navy - the Dreadnaught. Along with close friends (including the famous Virginia Woolf) he sent word that

Prince Makalen of Abbysinia wished to view the ship.

Upon arrival, the group spoke in gibberish, and bestowed fake 'foreign' honours on the captain and crew of the vessel.

Throughout the tour, they would exclaim their amazement at some part of the ship with the phrase "Bunga Bunga!". When the whole prank became public knowledge, the Navy was ridiculed utterly.

Clearly black-face and such exclamations would not fly in today's more politically correct world, and quite reasonably so. However, at the time it was considered the height of hilarity, apparently. You only have to watch 1970's British television to know how long this sort of humour lasted.

The upshot was that British naval officers had "Bunga Bunga!" shouted at them in the street, and the phrase even made it into a popular song of the time.

> *When I went on board a Dreadnought ship*
> *I looked like a costermonger;*
> *They said I was an Abyssinian prince*
> *'Cos I shouted 'Bunga Bunga!'*

It was probably quite lucky that Cole and his compatriots were not arrested for the whole affair, though the Navy were more than a little aggrieved about the whole thing and were definitely pushing for it. Cole and friends (except for Virginia Woolf) were subject to a "symbolic thrashing of the buttocks" by junior naval officers. A penalty which would likely be considered ludicrous by today's standards.

Alas, karma finally caught up with Cole. He lost all his money in Canadian land speculation, his marriage failed, and he died more or less alone in France, of a heart attack.

Throughout the tour, they would exclaim their amazement at some part of the ship with the phrase "Bunga Bunga!". When the whole prank became public knowledge, the Navy was ridiculed utterly.

DIOGENES (AROUND 400 BC)

I like to think I'm a cynical sod. It comes with the territory... but there are cynics and there are cynics, and Diogenes was about as cynical as it is possible to get. He was a Greek philosopher from around 412 BC. He was not the most pleasant of individuals.

He was certainly a remarkable man, if the tales are to be believed. I think he was obstreperous, unreasonable, and irritating. Plato (another famous philosopher of the age, who you are far more likely to have heard of) almost certainly considered him a villain.

EXILE AND OUTCAST
Not a great deal is known about the early years of Diogenes, and his upbringing. He is believed to have been the son of a banker, in Sinope, a city on the edge of the Black Sea, and was involved in the

banking industry himself.

He became enmeshed in a scandal involving the defacing and devaluing of currency, and as a result, he was stripped of all material possessions and assets. He was exiled from Sinope, his citizenship revoked, and his reputation in absolute tatters.

Currency fraud was a real problem at the time. Money, and minting thereof, was still a fairly new art form, and when the powers-that-be hammered down on perceived currency devaluation, you can bet that they weren't going to be playing nice. It is interesting that they felt that exile and asset stripping was a crueller punishment than execution.

HOMELESSNESS IN ATHENS

Somewhat at a loss as to what he should do now, Diogenes visited the Oracle at Delphi. Whatever he was told there convinced him that he should continue to live in austerity, and challenge the fundamental tenets of society, which he saw as flawed and lacking in moral character.

Nothing changes, I guess. Pretty much all the complaints about society are the same ones that have been made since complaints were first written down. Case in point, Plato - who also appears later in this tale - is often attributed as once having said:

> *"The children now love luxury; they have bad manners, contempt for authority; they show disrespect for elders and love chatter in place of exercise. Children are now tyrants, not the servants of their households. They no longer rise when elders enter the room. They contradict their parents, chatter before company, gobble up dainties at the table, cross their legs, and tyrannize their teachers."*

Now tell me you've not heard similar - from two and a half thousand years ago - in recent decades?

It's not long after this that Diogenes got rid of every earthly possession. He lived naked inside an over-turned clay wine barrel (bigger than you might expect), and... regressed. He ate in the marketplace (a social *faux pas* at the time), piddled on people who insulted him, crapped in the theatre, and even masturbated in public.

> *I fawn on those who give me anything, I yelp at those who refuse, and I set my teeth in rascals.*
> *- Diogenes*

As a bit of a party trick, he would wander around the market during bright daylight with a lit lamp, and when anyone asked him what he was doing, he would shout that he was "looking for an honest man!"

In short, he was the sort of person that other people warn you about on local community groups on social media. You know... the whole "Watch out, the creepy old guy who wears a beanbag for trousers is hanging around outside the supermarket again, flinging poo at beagle owners."

FEUD WITH PLATO

Diogenes certainly wasn't the only philosopher in Athens. The place was positively dripping with them. You couldn't walk more than a few paces in any given direction without someone with a name like a cut-price ointment trying to tell you how to live your life.[53]

There's a lot to be said for a society that prized mental exercise... and some of the foundations of modern thought came out of this place and time... but sometimes you have to wonder how anyone got any work done.

Plato is widely considered one of the most important and influential individuals in human history and carved quite the niche in the history of Ancient Greek and Western philosophy.

Diogenes didn't like him one bit.

Diogenes used to feed packs of wild dogs in the city, and he would turn up to Plato's classes and set the dogs loose, causing mayhem.

He would loudly argue with Plato during class, and even once arrived with a plucked chicken, and shouted "Look, Plato! I have brought you a man!" - as a means of mocking one of Plato's famous definitions of humanity.

One of Plato's big ticket philosophical items was his theory of ideals. "There are" he would say "many cups, but only one idea of 'cupness'." - That is, there is an ideal of a cup, from which all other cups have sprung.

This is actually something which is quite useful in terms of artificial intelligence and machine learning at the moment, so it's shown itself to be quite an interesting school of thought, even if your initial reaction is to scratch your head and go "Wuh?"

Diogenes openly mocked the idea, and suggested that as the cup Plato was using as an example was empty, there must be a fundamental idea of 'emptiness', tapped Plato on the forehead and said, "I think you will find here is the emptiness".

Then he pissed on Plato's stool and ran away.

It was certainly not his only interaction with his rival, and there is no doubt that Plato would likely have wanted to clock him one right in the kisser for the stool, if nothing else. I have to wonder what amazing insights into thought and being that Plato may have come up with, if it wasn't for Diogenes sitting in the sidelines going "Ner! Ner! Ner-Ner! Ner!" every five minutes.

SLAVERY AND ALEXANDER THE GREAT

At some point in his life, Diogenes was captured by pirates and sold into slavery, to a Corinthian named Xeniades. It's not entirely clear what happened at this point, but it didn't take long for Xeniades to let him go ... which is potentially a testament to his overall... charisma. (Char*isn't*ma?)

Apparently, he found an overturned clay wine barrel to live in while in Corinth (Greece), too, and there is a record of Diogenes lying naked in the sun in outside of it when Alexander the Great walked by with several of his inner circle.

He is said to have looked down upon Diogenes and asked, "Can I help you with something?" - bearing in mind that this was, at the time, one of the most powerful human beings to ever walk the Earth.

Diogenes responded with something pithy, and not a little rude, which is remarkably similar to "Yeah, you can get out of my sun." - fortunately for him, Alexander seemed to find this amusing, and left him to it, with the parting shot "But truly, if I were not Alexander, I wish I were Diogenes." - a tale which is recorded several times by different sources, with a few differences in each telling, and may be apocryphal.

THE END OF DIOGENES

There are several stories which talk about how Diogenes died.

Some tales say he died of an infected dog bite. Others say he ate a raw octopus and got sick. One or two even claim he just got fed up one day and held his breath until he died... which is unlikely. My money's on the octopus.

Some claim that he demanded his corpse be thrown outside the city walls to be eaten by wild animals.

Either way... if the tales are accurate, he lived well into his eighties, and whether you consider him a villain, or one of the fathers of philosophical cynicism, he was certainly a remarkable character.

None of his writings remain, though he is believed to have written at least ten works on the subject which were discussed by others including, ironically, Plato. We know him mainly through references by other authors at the time.

BÁTHORY ERZSÉBET (1550-1614)

Whether horrific vampire-styled serial killer, or victim of a political conspiracy, the question of Báthory Erzsébet (aka Elizabeth Báthory) is perplexing and obscured by lurid tales of torture and blood.

Báthory was born in 1560 in Hungary to family who were among the highest ranking in Transylvania. She may have been epileptic, one of the 'cures' for which at the time was consumption of blood and bone of a non-sufferer... this becomes important later.

Tales say that she was surrounded by brutality and cruelty as she grew, witnessing the horrific punishments meted out by her father's soldiery, amid rumours of Satanism and witchcraft.

After marriage in the late 1500s, Báthory moved into her husband's estate in the

Little Carpathians. With her husband frequently away fighting the Ottomans, Elizabeth Báthory managed all his business affairs and the upkeep of the estates. She was responsible for the welfare of the local villages.

When her husband died some years later, she became hugely wealthy in her own right.

As the 17th century started, horrific rumours emerged about Báthory and her estate. Rumours that involved torture, murder, and bathing in the blood of victims. Arranged by Báthory and facilitated by loyal servants.

Báthory is said to have been murdering the daughters of lower-ranked nobility, who were sent to her castle to learn courtly etiquette. The death toll had reportedly reached over 650 victims.

The king sent high-ranking official György Thurzó to investigate rumours. He started by canvasing the area for those who were willing to testify against Báthory... the legal system of the day being somewhat less constrained by such things as 'reliable evidence' as it is today. He started with 52 'witnesses' and ended up with over three hundred.

Most of the witnesses stated outright that they had heard the accusations from others but did not see it themselves. Several confessed under torture, which - let's face it - is hardly a reliable way to extract information from anyone, because after a certain point you'll just scream whatever you think your accuser wants to hear.

According to the tales, György Thurzó and his men raided the castle and found Báthory covered in blood. In point of fact, she was seated for dinner, and such lurid nonsense was invented by the 17th century equivalent of the tabloid press.

Subsequent trials found Báthory guilty, and she was confined for the rest of her life to her castle under strict lockdown. Her servants - who had been tortured - were executed.

Thurzó himself stated that Báthory was locked in a single brick room, but it appears she had free run of the castle and grounds, as long as she was accompanied... so more of a house arrest.

Modern historians have argued that Elizabeth Báthory was a victim of a conspiracy, with proceedings against her deemed politically motivated due to her wealth. Thurzó also had political ambitions that would have been advanced with the removal of Báthory from her position.

So, we go from the enduring tales of Báthory's villainy due to bathing in her virgin victims' blood to retain her beauty or youth... or the villainy of political monsters building a fraudulent case against a noblewoman for personal and political gain.

Likely a situation which has spent far too long being warped by historical liberty-taking to ever be reliably explored.

Báthory was found dead in her chambers in August 1614. She was originally buried in the nearby Church of Csejte until superstitious villagers complained. Eventually, her body was relocated to her birth home at Ecsed, in Hungary, and its present location is unknown.

LEONARDA EMILIA (1842-1873)

As far as nicknames go, this lady had a good one. My nickname was one of the minor characters from the Asterix cartoons. I had a mate who was called Beans for over 20 years, because once, just once, he had string beans in his lunchbox in primary school. "La Carambada" really earned her nickname.

Born Leonarda Emilia, in Mexico in 1842, she met and fell in love with a French soldier during the Second French Intervention in Mexico.

This is basically when the Second French Empire invaded Mexico (1861-1867) - during this period there were a fair few French soldiers around, and Mexico City was at one point captured by the French forces. It's a fascinating era in history, and I recommend some light reading, even if it's only Wikipedia.

When the war ended, Leonarda's French beau decided not to go back to France with the armies, and instead remained with her in Mexico.

Unfortunately, anti-French sentiments were high, and he was taken prisoner by local loyalists. Even though Leonarda pleaded for his release (and his only crime was presumably that he was French in a land that had recently been attacked by the French) he was executed.

For most people, the tale would have ended there, but Leonarda was not about to let this go.

Adopting the name La Carambada, "The Amazing Lady", Leonarda learned how to ride, shoot, fight, and use a gun. Then, having gained rage-fuelled expertise in the art of guerrilla warfare, she began her reign of terror.

Her methods were... questionable at best.

What we do know for sure is that her reign of terror saw her become the leader of a crime syndicate. She and her men would rob rich travellers around Querétaro and Guanajuato, roughly 236 miles (380km) north-west of Mexico City.

These travellers would frequently be carrying large quantities of silver from the famed silver mines in the area, so pickings were good.

While she has been compared with Robin Hood

for a tendency to steal from the rich and give to the poor, the source material is a rather romanticised ballad - and it's hard to know how true-to-life the claims were.

She would also murder corrupt government officials whenever she found them... though corruption was determined largely by hearsay and guesswork, so... well, if you were a government official, you could pretty much just roll the dice.

Needless to say, she had no love of the Mexican Government of the day.

As she wore men's clothing during her raids, she would flash her breasts at defeated and robbed travellers to shame them with the knowledge that they had been beaten by a woman.

I mean, she could have just told them, but I guess that just wouldn't have had the same impact. Macho culture of the time would have given this quite the sting. I'm assuming that she never bothered to do this to the government officials that she had just killed, because there probably wouldn't be much point.

Much of Leonarda's tale is lost to history, but there are claims that she gained her final revenge by poisoning the men who - years previously - had ignored her pleas and had her French lover executed: The provincial governor and the then

Mexican president.

Certainly, President Benito Juárez did die at around the right time (1872) for this to be true - though his cause of death is recorded as a heart attack.

This part of the tale is therefore likely apocryphal, but certainly not beyond the realms of possibility. It has a narrative symmetry which is hard to ignore, either way... and would almost certainly be the culmination of any movie of Leonarda's escapades, even if it wasn't historically accurate.

Alas, Leonarda's end was untimely, but not unexpected for someone who lived by the blade and the bullet. She was shot - hit by five bullets - during a confrontation with government forces in 1873. She confessed her story to a priest while on her deathbed, and passed away in Police custody, at the age of 31.

SIGURD EYSTEINSSON (872-892 AD)

They're a hardy bunch in the Orkney and Shetland Islands... those twisted little outcrops of rock just off the northern Scottish coast. Here we find Sigurd the Mighty, a Viking who was killed by a dead man.

Sigurd inherited an earldom and the Orkney and Shetland islands over a thousand years ago, when the Viking scourge (for indeed, if you were not a Viking, they were a smidge scourgey) was an ever-present danger.

It was originally the domain of his brother Rognvald, who had been awarded it by both right of conquest, and the Norwegian king. Rognvald really didn't give a damn, however, and had other irons in various fires, so he left the lot with his younger brother, Sigurd, and scarpered off elsewhere.[54]

Sigurd was quite happy to become the earl, and lorded it over his islands like... well, I guess a lord.[55]

The thing is, he wasn't content to just stay on the islands and earl. While he could earl with the best of them, he cast his eyes further south, to the ... (dramatic music) ... Land of the Scots!

So, a-raiding they could go, taking riches and having adventures, and his exploits in conquering the north of Scotland became part of the *Orkneyinga Saga*, a sort-of collected works of the Orkney and Shetland islands mythos.

As the tale goes, not far from the mouth of the *River Oykel* in Scotland, Sigurd challenged the local warlord - an ugly fellow with the somewhat apt name of *Máel Brigte the Buck-Toothed* - to battle.

While the local warlords would certainly fight amongst themselves back in the grim dawn of Scottish history (which could, let's be fair, be any time between 400 AD and last Tuesday) they would happily unite in great numbers to fight off the boaty buggers from across the water... so Sigurd neatly sidestepped this by appealing to Máel's pride.

> *"Could you beat us if we were evenly matched? I don't think so."*

Of course, Máel couldn't turn down the chance

to prove him wrong, so the two leaders agreed to a battle of forty men each to decide who would rule the local area. Máel picked his forty bravest warriors, kitted them out in the best gear they could find, and they trudged to the battleground showing their best fighting spirit...

... where Sigurd was waiting with his entire raiding force of eighty men.

To say the battle was a little one-sided was perhaps understating it. Sigurd's victory was complete, and as a final act, he beheaded *Máel Brigte the Buck-Toothed* and tied the detached noggin to the saddle of his horse by its long black hair.

Rounding up his men, Sigurd led the Viking force back to their encampment.

The gruesome head bounced and boinged like a filth-encrusted Gàidhlig yoyo, and those very buck-teeth which had earned Máel Brigte his name contrived to bite Sigurd on his shapely Scandiwegian thigh.

The bite - probably more of a dirty scratch, under the circumstances - became infected and, antibiotics not being a thing yet[56], Sigurd became sick, and died before they could return home.

Sigurd's death left a trail of disorder back in the Islands. At first his son became ruler, but he died only a few months in. Then Rognvald turned up again and made his son the ruler... but he got his backside handed to him by pirates and fled back to Norway in disgrace. Finally, a frustrated Rognvald appointed the son of his concubine (and slave) to the seat, more out of desperation than anything, and order was ultimately restored.

To say the battle was a little one-sided was perhaps understating it. Sigurd's victory was complete, and as a final act, he beheaded Máel Brigte the Buck-Toothed and tied the detached noggin to the saddle of his horse by its long black hair.

NICOLAS FERRIAL (1479-1536)

All the world loathes a smartass, and a jester is just a villain in a silly hat as far as I'm concerned. Don't mistake me, they're not as bad as mimes (spit) but there's a special place in hell reserved for the jingly hat-wearing jongleurs of jocularity.

Ferrial was a special sort of jester. He was a court jester to French royalty. He may have had a quick wit, but he was never short of an enemy or two. He has more attributed to him than he probably accomplished, but that is the way of historical figures.

Ferrial managed to royally ('scuse pun) piss off King Louis XII. While performing his duties as a jester, Ferrial got lost in the moment and walloped the king on his somewhat ample backside.

Now... there are a number of reasons why whacking the king on the bum is a Bad Thing (tm) but this one was very nearly his undoing.

The king was - in the parlance of the kids of today – *"miffed AF"* and ordered Ferrial hanged by the neck until dead. Ferrial was naturally more than a little worried by this proclamation - but the King was not without mercy. He said that if Ferrial could think of an apology which was more offensive than the offending deed, that he would let Ferrial off with a warning.

Ferrial's response was:

> *"I apologise, your majesty. I didn't recognise you.*
> *I mistook you for the Queen."*

He may be a lowly jester with impulse control issues, but he certainly had some big brass jongleurs.

Now, you might think his tale ends here, but it doesn't. Because he had developed a bit of a reputation for poking fun at the un-poke-funables (the monarchy), King Francis I passed down an edict. This edict was "If you take the piss out of me, I'll knock your block off".

In other words, using the monarch as the butt of your jokes would result in your execution. Ferrial managed some offence - though it's not clear what that was - and the King was furious. Ferrial was to be executed, but in recognition of his long years of service, the monarch said that Ferrial could choose the manner of his own death.

Ferrial thought long and hard, and once again, his weasely villainous jocular brain came up with:

> *Bon sire, par sainte Nitouche et*
> *saint Pansard, patrons de la folie,*
> *je demande à mourir de vieillesse.*

This translates loosely to:

> *Old age, please.*

The king, hoist by his own petard at this point, commuted the sentence of death, and ordered that Ferrial could not, under any circumstances, be executed.

The whole affair was not without consequence, however... Ferrial was kicked out of the kingdom for the rest of his life. Ferrial - and his pseudonym Triboulet - appear in several plays and operas which have occurred subsequent, so it's not like he didn't have his fair share of admirers.

GIUSEPPE MARCO FIESCHI. (1790-1836)

King Louis-Philippe ruled over France for 18 years from 1830 onwards and goes down in history as being the last king of France. He was a bit of a conservative, a coloniser, and oversaw the French conquest of Algeria. He was forced to abdicate during the French Revolution of 1848 and lived the rest of his life in Exile in England.

He very nearly didn't do most of that, because Giuseppe Marco Fieschi tried to assassinate him in 1835.

As far as kings go, Louis-Philippe wasn't as bad as all that, if you weren't on the receiving end of his conquering or colonial aspirations... (if you were, then that's a whole different story) ... but his system of justice had previously sentenced Fieschi to ten years in prison - and Fieschi didn't think this was very fair at all.

For stealing a cow.

A lifetime of theft, fraud, and forging on Fieschi's part apparently didn't factor into his thinking in this regard - but needless to say, he was adamant he didn't steal the cow... and was a bit snippy about the whole thing. As a result, he was quite adamant that the king should be rendered.... um.... functionally inanimate.

Now, our lad Fieschi - apart from a brief stint as a shepherd in Corsica - had spent a lot of time flitting about in military garb shooting at things and therefore knew his way around a firearm.

He figured that the best way to ensure the end of the king was through the careful application of gunpowder, a small lead ball, and enough of a distance to beat a hasty retreat before the King's guards could go "Hey!" and chase after him.

Being a bit worried about missing, and not wanting to make a hash of it, he had a cunning plan. It was, as Blackadder once said:

> *...a plan so cunning you could pin a tail on it and call it a weasel!*

Unfortunately, it was also a very poorly conceived plan.

With a number of accomplices, and the generous donation of 500 francs from similarly inclined king-haters, Fieschi built a 25-barrel 'volley gun' -

each barrel being loaded with eight lead balls.

It wasn't exactly a well-machined marvel of the modern industrial age... think of a rack with 25 thin pipes stuck to it, and you'll get the idea.

This was mounted inside a building on the route the King was known to take periodically during parades.

On July 28, 1835, Fieschi loaded the volley gun and waited until the King was crossing the street.

With a loud 'BANG!', around four-hundred red-hot balls of lead flew from the gun(s) and raced down the Boulevard du Temple. Every single one of them missed the king and his family, but managed to kill eighteen other people, and injure twenty-two more in the crowd around him.

It was a bit like shooting fish in a barrel, only to find you'd shot not only the wrong barrel, but that it wasn't in-fact a barrel at all, but some kind of grandfather clock, and the fish (some distance away in an actual barrel) were now merely slightly startled.

So poorly did the firearm work, that Fieschi - who, we must remember, was standing behind it at the time - was also hit, resulting in severe injuries. As he couldn't scarper, he was captured very quickly indeed.

Fieschi was very surprised to find that the King

insisted he receive the best medical care, and he was nursed back to health in prison. Being a fine, upstanding criminal, he decided to name every single one of his aides and accomplices, certain that the King would - after having spared no expense having him healed - simply banish him.

Fieschi was even more surprised when the King instead sentenced him to the guillotine for attempted regicide. Fieschi's volley gun, which became known as the *Machine Infernale*, is now part of the collection of the *Musée des Archives Nationales* in Paris.

EDWARD DRAX FREE (1764-1843)

There comes a time in every young lad's life when he looks back upon his collected works and thinks "What set of terrible decisions brought me here? Perhaps I should have moved to Craggy Island and become a priest." - but sometimes Real Life is far more outrageous than Father Ted... and Reverend Drax Free was certainly a fine example.

Born in 1764 in England, Edward Drax Free attended St Johns College, Oxford, but while a gifted student, he spent more time chasing chambermaids than he spent chasing his studies. Nevertheless, he completed a Master of Arts degree, and became a Doctor of Divinity...and was appointed Vicar of St Giles' Church, Oxford.

His somewhat scandalous nature - full of wine, women, and song - was almost his downfall at this time, and in 1808, he was just about to be kicked out when he landed himself the role of Rector of the Church of All Saints, Sutton, Bedfordshire.

So, moving to Bedfordshire - in what was likely to have been the clergy's equivalent of him being 'dressed for export', you'd think that Free might have learned his lesson, and started to toe the clergy line in order to keep his job.

In point of fact, this is not what happened. His sermons were few, but unpardonably profane. He was accused of stealing lead off his own church roof to pay for his vices.

He allowed pigs to run free in the graveyard, causing damage, and toppling gravestones. He argued with parishioners, often while drunk, and was open about his collection of "gentlemen's special-interest literature".

He also continued to chase chambermaids and housekeepers, producing with some enthusiasm at least five illegitimate children. In the end, he used to lock the church on a Sunday to keep the patrons out, because he quite simply couldn't be bothered with all that religious malarkey. This went on for some years, and it is only because he happened to piss off the wrong member of the landed gentry that things eventually came to a head.

There were issues over a burial in the vault of the Burgoynes family, and the wealthy head of the household (Montagu Burgoyne, a well-known politician) laid a complaint on behalf of the whole village in 1830.

Edward was soon stripped of his title, and ordered to vacate the church... but refused. When his removal was to be enforced by a group of heavies sent by the local bishop, Edward locked himself in the rectory with a favourite chambermaid, several barrels of wine, and two pistols.

A tense stand-off developed, and the bishop's men basically had to lay siege to the rectory. This went on for at least two weeks, until - finally out of claret - Edward gave himself up.

Without a job or an income, Edward fell on hard times in a period of history that was not particularly well-renowned for looking after the indigent. He died penniless and alone some 13 years later... having been run over in the street by a varnish-manufacturer's horse-drawn cart.

EVARISTE GALOIS (1811-1832)

But the flash of thought is like the sun -- sudden, absolute: Watch at the desk, through the window raised on the flawless dark, the hand that trembles in the light, Lucid, sudden. Until the sun I have no time.

- Antiphon for Evariste Galois, by Carol Drake (1957)

It's tough to read about a life cut short when the person involved had so much to offer the world. How much humanity could have gained, the strides we could have made, had this person lived even a few more years beyond the short twenty that were allotted him. Evariste Galois is one such person... so settle in for a tragic tale.

Born in France, his father was the mayor of Bourg-la-Reine. His mother was responsible for his early education, and it's clear she knew what she was doing. Galois took an interest in mathematics from a very early age.

In 1828 he applied for entrance to the most prestigious French institution for mathematics – the *École Polytechnique*. He was rebuffed because, even though he scored rather well in the exam, he could not explain how he knew things.[57] He had the logic, but not the language of (what was then) modern mathematics. His expertise was instinctual, rather than learned, and his brilliance did not translate through the rigid bureaucratic structure of the entrance examination process.

Consigned to a 'lesser' school, *l'École Préparatoire*, he nevertheless published his first paper about fractions, and made some fundamental inroads into the theory of polynomial equations. Something which, alas, eludes me to this day.

His father committed suicide on the eve of his second attempt at entering *École Polytechnique* (after an argument with a priest) and Galois – understandably - failed again... this time quite blatantly because of the incompetent examiner's lack of understanding of Galois' new approach to solving mathematical problems. Galois snapped and, in a rage, said a few things which certainly did not endear him to the school's administration – but ultimately had to return to *l'École*

Préparatoire instead.

It was Galois political leanings that got him into notable trouble initially, and almost certainly resulted in his eventual downfall.

In the early days of the 1800s, France was a political mess. Revolution was in the air, and it didn't look like much was going to stop it. During an attempted government coup, the students of the prestigious *École Polytechnique* were out on the street raising hell, whereas the students of *l'École Préparatoire* were locked inside their stone building... possibly for their own safety... but Galois was livid, and later wrote a scathing opinion piece which – in modern parlance – tore the school's director a new one.

Galois was therefore expelled from the only mathematical school that would have him.

So he joined the politically active artillery unit of the National Guard, which had expressed strong pro-republic political leanings, and was unsurprisingly soon thereafter disbanded because of worries that they might de-stabilise the government.

At a party not long afterwards, Galois proposed a toast to Louis Philippe, the king, during which he wielded a dagger in a menacing manner. Taken as a direct threat to the king[58], Galois was arrested... but acquitted due to having hired a rather good lawyer.

Nevertheless, not long afterwards, Galois put on the uniform of his old artillery unit, armed himself with pistols, rifle, and a dagger, and paraded the streets ostensibly looking for trouble... which he found in the form of yet another arrest.

He managed to get drunk in jail, and wrote a letter which basically said he missed his father, that he would probably die in a duel over a woman's honour, and – in short – screw the world, because everything sucked.[59]

He spent six months in prison, during which he eschewed his political affiliations in favour of mathematics.

While in prison, he received a review of his mathematical work from a noted French mathematician, which stated that it was "incomprehensible" with an argument that was "insufficiently clear".

This did not sit well with Galois, and history would prove him justified in being angry with what he considered to be a politically motivated review.

Upon his release from prison, Galois – for reasons largely unknown, but possibly linked to having rubbed certain individuals the wrong way – was talked into a duel to the death. Such things were relatively commonplace among the gentry, though technically illegal. There is some supposition based on his writings that he was coerced into the duel over a love affair gone awry. Galois himself wrote:

> *I am the victim of an infamous coquette and her two dupes!*[60]

His family later suggested the whole thing had been arranged surreptitiously by royalists, and the Police at the time, to eliminate a political enemy... and it was certainly not unheard of for such a thing to occur. Having said that, Galois was merely an angry lad with a mathematical gift and was unlikely to have qualified for singling out in such a convoluted manner.

Galois was sure he was going to be killed, so he spent the entire night writing out everything he knew about mathematics, gathered all his old treatises and papers, and bound them together into a single mathematical testament, which he sent to his friend Auguste Chevalier.

It was prefaced with the haunting phrase "I have no time".

Early in the morning of 30 May 1832, Evariste Galois was shot in the stomach. He was left in the field to die by his opponents (and his own seconds) and found late in the afternoon by a passing farmer. He died the following morning of peritonitis.

Years later in 1843, his manuscript was reviewed and declared not only 'sound', but 'exceptional'. It contained novel proofs to mathematical problems, and his methods led to the development of Galois Theory, which I am given to understand is brilliant, but far beyond my limited mathematical understanding. He had also founded a vastly important branch of algebra known as *group theory* and added considerably to knowledge of continued fractions.

> *This letter, if judged by the novelty and profundity of ideas it contains, is perhaps the most substantial piece of writing in the whole literature of mankind.*
> *- Mathematician Hermann Weyl, University of Göttingen*

For a lad who died in a duel, aged 20, he left an incredibly enduring legacy. Just imagine what he could have achieved had he lived on, past the excesses of youth, past the surge of hormonal angst and through the grief of familial loss, into a quieter, perhaps more cerebral part of life, where he could have explored the rapidly unfolding possibilities of 'new mathematics'.

His last words to his crying brother were

Ne pleure pas, Alfred! J'ai

*besoin de tout mon courage
pour mourir à vingt ans!*

*Don't cry, Alfred. I need all my
courage to die at twenty.*

JUAN PUJOL GARCIA (1912-1988)

It was World War II, and Europe was in tatters. The German war machine had ploughed a huge furrow across the continent, and had its sights set on Britain... but a lonely little Spaniard stood up and said "No more!"

EARLY LIFE

Juan "Pujol" Garcia was born in Barcelona in 1912. He worked as a chicken farmer, and as a cinema manager until the 1930s[61], wherein he was forced to join the Republican cavalry under Spain's pre-war policy of compulsory military service.

He was not a good soldier and bounced in and out of military service for a while, with "AWOL" and arrest thrown in periodically for good measure.

He was opposed to the Republican ideology during the Spanish civil war, so defected to the Nationalists. However, he discovered that they were pro-fascist, which he realised he hated far more than he hated the pro-communist Republican ideals.

He managed to survive the civil war quite proud of the fact that he had not fired a single bullet in anger... but the entire experience left him detesting both German and Russian ideologies in general... which set him up well for the start of World War II.

WORLD WAR II

When the war began, and Germany and Russian forces began their relentless march across Europe, Juan Pujol Garcia decided that he had to do something... but fighting wasn't the something he wanted to do.

He offered himself as an agent to Britain, through the British embassy in Madrid... but they had no need of an amateur spy and told him so in no uncertain terms. He tried three times. They rebuffed him three times.

So, he decided to try a different tack.

He approached the Germans, pretending to be a fanatically pro-Nazi Spanish government official and asked them if they would like a spy... and they said "Sure". They trained him, paid him, and gave him instructions to move to London and recruit a network of spies, to feed information back to German High Command.

THE SPY NETWORK

Instead, he moved to Lisbon, and purchased a copy of The Tourist's Guide to Britain. He then sat down and created screeds of information based on regular news reports, cine-reels, and rumour, which completely fooled his German handlers.

Furthermore, he created an entirely fake network of espionage agents across the whole of Britain - all of whom provided regional information (naturally, through Pujol) which became known throughout German High Command as one of the most extensive networks under their control, and of huge significance to the war effort.

Bear in mind that, at this point, Pujol was not providing them with anything that hadn't already hit a newspaper or film reel.

British Intelligence (MI5) found out about Pujol, and were hugely concerned, and the knowledge sparked a major spy hunt to try to winkle out members of the network. Pujol had everyone fooled.

MI5, however, didn't take too long to realise that feeding the Germans misinformation was a great idea, and that Pujol was working (for himself) against the Axis powers.[62]

Furthermore, Pujol had so many fake agents operating in the UK that the Germans were overwhelmed by the sheer amount of intelligence coming out of them. All of it from Pujol's own hand, it seems. This stopped them from attempting to recruit more agents... which meant that their greatest source of information was... quite frankly... a load of cobblers.

WORKING WITH MI5

Eventually, MI5 was able to contact Pujol, and work with him to create even greater acts of misinformation for the German war effort.

With MI5's aid, Pujol was able to provide the Germans with very real information about troop movements and shipping... all just a tiny little bit too late... so that the Germans were actually apologising to Pujol for getting there too late, but were praising him on the quality of his information.

Some of the details of the invasion of Normandy... D-Day... were provided to Germany via Pujol and his fake spy network... all the time ensuring that it was just too late to do anything useful about it... cementing his value as a trusted source.

Then, when D-Day actually launched, Pujol informed the Germans that it was a feint, intended to draw troops away from the actual landing place... helping to convince Hitler and his cronies that the attack was actually still some days away, and much further to the north.

It worked so well that the Germans kept two full armoured divisions and 19 infantry divisions in the Pas de Calais waiting for a second invasion. This greatly weakened the German's ability to react to the invasion, saved countless lives, and almost certainly shortened the war.

Still, before the war ended, the Germans went so far as to award Pujol with an Iron Cross, a very prestigious military honour. Only four months later, he received an MBE from King George VI.

After the war, and fearing German loyalist reprisal, Pujol faked his own death, moved to Venezuela, and lived out the rest of his life as a bookstore owner. He died in 1988 in Caracas.

HETTY GREEN (1834-1916)

The name 'Scrooge' from the character Ebenezer Scrooge in Charles Dickens' A Christmas Carol (1843) has become synonymous with penny-pinching and stinginess. Perhaps, however, instead of 'Scrooge', we should use 'Hetty'?

Hetty Green was born in 1834 in Massachusetts, USA. She was the daughter of an extremely wealthy whaler and China trader, and certainly didn't want for money. Money, however, seems to be all that she wanted... if that makes any sense. She is recorded in history as being almost pathologically miserly.

In her early 20s, her father died and left her around six million dollars. That's $101 million in today's money, and a more-than reasonable fortune by just about anyone's standards I'm sure you'll agree.

Shortly thereafter, an aunt died, with an estate valued at around $2 million ($33 million in today's money), and left half of it to Hetty. She left the other half to charity.

Hetty, in a profound display of what I would consider to be extreme scumbaggery, challenged the will's validity in court. That's not the bad bit... the bad bit is that she forged parts of an earlier will to invalidate any subsequent wills. Essentially lying to claw money back from the charities, and to line her own pockets.

Why she didn't do time for this I don't know... but I assume it was something to do with being extremely wealthy.

Leaving fraud aside, she was a savvy and patient investor, to be sure. In her own words:

> *I buy when things are low and nobody wants them. I keep them until they go up and people are crazy to get them. That is, I believe, the secret of all successful business.*
> *- Hetty Green*

She became known as the "Queen of Wall Street", and her fortune grew and grew... as did her reputation for... well, politely put it would be 'thriftiness'.

She never spent money on soap, survived on a diet that was primarily fifteen-cent pies, never turned on the hot water or heating, and at one point is said to have spent half a night searching her (ancient, breakdown old) carriage for a lost stamp worth two cents.

While very-much the effective businesswoman, she did not rent her own offices, preferring to work out of the basement of a bank, surrounded by her trunks and suitcases, and lived in a variety of boarding houses to avoid paying New York property tax.

She wore a single black dress until it wore out, before buying another one, and her somewhat dour look was likely to be the reason for the later nickname "The Witch of Wall Street".

> *Just because I dress plainly and do not spend a fortune on my gowns, they say I am cranky or insane.*
> *- Hetty Green*

She makes a good point, though the contesting of her aunt's will certainly sets her on the path of villainy... but the big kicker ('scuse pun)... was her son's leg.

Ned, her son, broke his leg. How this happened is not recorded, but by all accounts, it was a bad break. Rather than pay for a doctor, Hetty spent considerable time finding a free clinic. Upon entering the free clinic, and starting treatment, her identity was established, and it was insisted that she pay. Instead of paying, she took her son and fled, and attempted to treat the injury herself.

Eventually, infection set in, and Ned's leg had to be amputated... because Hetty refused to pay for a doctor.

Her extreme frugality didn't just affect poor Ned, however. She took great interest in her daughter's suitors, and refused to let her marry until a suitor was able to bring $2 million to the marriage, and even then, forced a prenuptial agreement on the pair.

Upon her death in 1916 at the age of 81, Hetty had an estimated net worth ranging from $100 million to $200 million (equivalent to $2.38 billion to $4.76 billion in today's money), making her arguably the richest woman in the world at the time.

She clearly had a keen mind and remarkable ability to turn a profit... but her early forgery and later child-damaging miserliness hints at neurological problems, potentially resulting in business practices which would absolutely be considered unethical and at-best morally suspect in today's society.

Her financial expertise was absolutely recognised, and while she had the nickname "The Witch of Wall Street", upon her death she was also known as "The Wizard of Finance'.

Her daughter, Sylvia - who eventually inherited

most of the money of the Green estate - was not so miserly. Upon her death in 1948, the $200 million remaining was split among dozens of colleges, churches, hospitals, and other charities.

She never spent money on soap, survived on a diet that was primarily fifteen-cent pies, never turned on the hot water or heating, and at one point is said to have spent half a night searching her (ancient, breakdown old) carriage for a lost stamp worth two cents.

JONAS HANWAY (1712-1786)

London. A city of vile stench, pea-soup fog, unbearable levels of disease and crime, and quite a lot of rain. A location, you would think, that would be ripe for the development of The Umbrella... but if you tried to open an umbrella in 18th century London, you would be lucky to escape without injury.

Consider the parasol. A delicate almost fairy-like cousin of the umbrella, this 'pretty' and often lacy device was used to shade women from the sun. London didn't get a lot of sun, and the device was known to hail mainly from France.

Back in the 1700s, the French and the English were... not chums. They had been at war on and off for centuries... and would be again... so any person who adopted a fashion which sprang from The Continent was to be sneered at and reviled in the same way you would revile someone who licked rat's bottoms for a hobby.

So, when Jonas Hanway, an English philanthropist and traveller, and noted opponent to tea drinking, decided he was sick of getting rained on, and procured himself an umbrella, he was in for a bit of a shock.

HANWAY IS RECORDED AS THE FIRST MALE LONDONER TO USE AN UMBRELLA.

Being dry, it seems, might be good enough for the French[63] but never for an Englishman. Moistness is character-building. Having a puddle of slightly grey rainwater pooling in your undergarments is a sign of high moral fibre.

Technically, women in London had been using parasols for years, and I'm sure that no small number made use of umbrellas during rain. It is therefore likely that umbrella use was seen as strictly feminine.

While the boundaries are certainly crumbling now, there was very much a strict demarcation between what was male and what was female back in the 1700s... so a man opening an umbrella... goodness me! It would be scarcely more scandalous if he'd whipped open his tweeds and run around Hyde Park helicoptering his gentleman-sausage at passers-by.

Men either got wet or stayed inside. They did NOT use an umbrella!

People literally threw rubbish at him. A driver of

a Hansom Cab clambered down from his vehicle and physically attacked him. (This was a tactical error, as Hanway was rather an accomplished pugilist, and not only defeated the Hansom Cab driver, but thrashed him soundly with said umbrella.) The cabbies in general were less than salutary about the situation.

The cabbies had an ulterior motive. If people were habitually bimbling about with umbrellas, they'd be less likely to take a cab to get from A to B. It was an interesting economic conundrum.

So, we now owe our ability to shield ourselves from drizzle thanks mainly to the stubborn efforts of Jonas Hanway and his insistence of sticking up for everyone's right to keep their hats dry.

In many ways, it is a shame that Hanway's fame largely involves the fact that he didn't want to moisten his chapeau. In his time, he founded The Marine Society, to keep up the supply of British seamen[64], and in 1758 he became a governor of the Foundling Hospital to look after deserted children. He helped found the Magdalen Hospital, and more... but you open one umbrella on a London street, and that's your goose cooked, mate.

Those of an enthusiastic English persuasion are perhaps more thankful that Hanway's campaign to ban tea drinking led to a somewhat less successful outcome. Then I'd be talking about him as a villain, and not about his erstwhile foldable not-get-wet device.

JOHN WESLEY HARDIN (1853-1895)

It's not called "The Wild West" for nothing. The formative years of the United States of America were a showcase in what happens when you've got a lot of land, and not a lot of law to oversee it. It also spawned heroes and villains with wild abandon.

Maybe not as famous as names like Billy the Kid, Jesse James, Butch & Sundance, or Snoot Burkle, but John Wesley Hardin is certainly among the more villainous outlaws the west ever saw.

Some of this is based on recorded historical fact, some comes from unverified claims made by Hardin himself. Take it all with a pinch of salt.

Early Life

Born in Texas in 1853, with a father who

was a traveling preacher, Hardin had a troubled childhood. At age nine he tried to run away to join the confederate army. At age 13 he got into a knife fight with another boy and left him almost dead.

It is when he turned 15, however, that he really started down his path as an outlaw. After a wrestling match with a former slave of his uncle, Hardin shot the man multiple times with a pistol. When the man died, Hardin's family sent him into hiding.

He was tracked down not long afterwards, and three Union soldiers were sent to arrest him. Believing they intended to kill him (which could actually have some basis in fact) he killed all three of them with a shotgun and a pistol.

The Outlaw

What followed was effectively an exercise in violence and thuggery, as he murdered his way back and forth across Texas as a fugitive, sometimes alone, sometimes in the company of other outlaws.

From shooting someone in the eye for a bottle of whiskey, to almost stereotypical killings over poker winnings, Hardin was quite thorough. Then, in 1871 he was arrested, briefly imprisoned, but managed to acquire a gun and kill four people while being transported to trial in Waco, Texas, and escaped again.

At this point, he was 17 years of age.[65]

Capture and escape did not change Hardin's lifestyle overmuch, and his killings continued. He killed a man by firing blindly through the wall of a hotel when the man was reportedly snoring too loud[66], and escaped with Wild Bill Hickok hot on his heels.

Capture and Imprisonment

He survived multiple further gunfights, skipping from town to town, before finally in 1877 - age 24 - half drunk, he was confronted by rangers while travelling on a train.

He attempted to draw his pistol, but it caught on his suspenders, and Hardin was knocked unconscious. He was tried and sentenced to 25 years in prison.

The tale doesn't end there of course.

After being caught trying to tunnel into the prison armoury, and multiple escape attempts, Hardin eventually found God[67], and plagued by ill-health, became a prison Sunday School teacher. He even wrote his autobiography.

> *Readers you see what drink and passion will do. If you wish to be successful in life, be temperate and control your passions; if you don't, ruin and death is the result. - Hardin*

Post Imprisonment

Against the odds, Hardin survived a lengthy incarceration, and was released in 1894. Later that year he passed the bar exam and acquired a licence to practice law.[68]

Not that this ended the shootings of course. Only a few years later, it is reported that he made a $5 bet that he could shoot a box and startle the sunbathing Mexican man who lay on top of it. He startled him alright. Fatally, unfortunately. Not from the bullet, which only hit the box... but from the fall, which left the poor man with a broken neck.

The End of Hardin

Hardin retired to El Paso and spent the rest of his life drinking and gambling. Things came to a head within a few years, when he exchanged heated words with a lawman who tried to arrest one of his female companions. This resulted in Hardin 'pistol whipping' the lawman and leaving him broken and bleeding in the street.

The following day, Hardin was relaxing, gambling, in the local saloon. The lawman's father entered, himself a former gunfighter and outlaw, and calmly walked up behind Hardin, and shot him in the back of the head.

Hardin's last words were reportedly "Four sixes to beat".

A lot of Hardin's claims as to his fights and conquests come from his autobiography, and he had a tendency to puff himself up a little. There are 16 or so confirmed shootings with which he was involved, and some 20 or more which he claimed but were unable to be verified. Even in prison he seems to have been overly concerned with his legend.

ANNA MARIA HELENA (1826-1908)

Born to a noble family, and styled Comtesse de Noailles, she did much to support the rights of women... but she was also an unusual eccentric, though some might style her a villain after she purchased a young girl in lieu of a painting.

Anna Maria was a wealthy English woman from a wealthy family. Money was never an issue, and she moved between her homes in England, and France as the seasons dictated.

She believed in a healthy mind supporting a healthy body and was not a fan of 'newfangled' technologies and science, and was vehemently opposed to - for example - vaccinations.

What she *did* believe, however, was that *air* was a

primary contributor towards health, and as such when the oak leaves began to fall, she would leave England for pastures new until the spring, as autumn and winter air were fundamentally *bad*.

She also believed that methane was remarkably healthy, and that the effluvial smell from the rear end of a cow was healthy in the extreme... and would ensure that a small herd of bovines was always outside her bedroom window, so that she could inhale deeply of the health-giving odours as she slept.

So far, a little odd, but 'remarkable'? She certainly had commendable qualities:

- She was a great believer in the rights of women in a time when debate was rife as to whether women should even be allowed to vote.
- She paid a great deal of money to support Elizabeth Blackwell during her struggle to become the first female doctor in the United States.
- She was a major shareholder in the controversial publication The English Women's Journal, dealing with women's welfare, employment, and equality.

So far, so good... but some folk might balk at the following:

The Painting and the Child

It was in Paris that she saw a painting by artist *Ernest Hébert* called *'Pasqua Maria'*. The painting was of a little girl standing demurely in a red peasant's dress.

Anna Maria loved the painting and viewed it on several occasions. It's not clear why she didn't purchase it - she certainly had the money - but she was somewhat dismayed when the painting was sold to Baron Rothschild and would no longer be available to be viewed publicly.

The girl *in* the painting however, had been a model on several occasions, including *Henriette Browne*'s 'Greek Captive' - so why she didn't buy one of these instead is perhaps a mystery.

Instead, she sought the parents of the child model, and purchased the child outright - supposedly for "two bags of gold" - which the parents agreed to on the understanding that the child would be raised as a Catholic and would never be painted again.

Anna Maria later adopted the child (*Maria Pasqua Abruzzesi*) as her own, and in all fairness likely did equip her for a better – or at least wealthier - life than she could have expected as a child of destitute Italian peasants.

The child was not brought up by Anna Maria, however, but instead was shipped off to a nearby convent school with strict conditions - enforced by financial penalties against the school should they not be met:

- The school pond was to be drained because ponds meant insects
- All trees were to be cut down
- Maria was to be dressed only in Greek style loose-fitting clothing, not the regular school uniform
- She would drink only milk... from a specific 'approved' cow.
- She was to be given an education according to Anna Maria's own priorities, rather than the standard curriculum
- She was not to wear lace shoes.

Anna Maria would visit her periodically, as the mood took her. It is not clear whether she took much of an interest beyond the aesthetic.

However - as an ornamental replacement for a favoured painting - Maria Pasqua was at least well educated, wanted for little that money could buy, and by all accounts continued her life happy and prosperous, outliving Anna Maria by over thirty years. She eventually married a doctor, and bore a daughter, who she named after her adoptive mother.

Later life and Death

Anna Maria, however, became rather more odd as she aged. There are some reports that she considered uncured squirrel and cat skins to be a cure against wrinkles, so had them sewn into her pyjamas ... and hung strings of onions from all the doorknobs - as a guard against general infection.

Upon her death, at the age of 82 (far ahead of the national average, so perhaps she was doing something right) she left a large financial endowment towards the construction of an orphanage.

It's arguable that she left the world a better place than she found it - something which you certainly can't say for everyone - and she was essentially a kind-hearted, if remarkably eccentric and somewhat aloof woman.

The thing is, Maria Pasqua later said that she had been happy with her life with her destitute parents, and being sold into what amounted to pampered eccentric slavery did not sit well with her as she grew into adulthood. It was a choice taken from her, and one of her lifelong regrets was never being able to return to the mountains of her homeland before she died in 1939.

JOHN HETHERINGTON (LATE 1700S – POSSIBLY APOCRYPHAL)

The late 1700s were not the most exciting of times. There was a fair bit going on, but there was no TV, no radio, and no internet. You couldn't go to the movies, and nobody had a phone. There were books, but reading was by no-means universal.

In short, if you were bored, you either found something to do, or you stayed bored. This is, perhaps, something that not many kids today appreciate. So, if something even remotely unusual happened - like someone inventing a new kind of cheese, or finding a better way of sharpening a pencil - the world went absolutely mental.

John Hetherington is a villain. Well, assuming someone who causes riots and is brought up on charges because of it, is a villain. How did he gain such notoriety? He wore a hat. Not just any hat. He invented the top hat. A large, shiny affair - the first of which he wore with aplomb as he strolled through the streets of London.

The crowd which formed behind him became so large and excited and dangerous that the authorities had to get involved and disperse them. Hetherington was scooped up and taken before the Lord Mayor.

He faced the Lord Mayor with the unusual charge of:

> *Walking down a public highway wearing upon his head a tall structure having a shining lustre calculated to alarm the people.*

It was claimed that women had fainted, children had gone into hysterics, and people had received broken bones as the chanting mob swelled and surged.

Hetherington was defiant and stood up for his right to dress as he saw fit, but the Lord Mayor - not willing to bow to the constraints of personal freedom - fined him £5,000. A sum worth somewhere in excess of £150,000 (US$18,800) in today's money.

Some claim the account is apocryphal - and it might well be, as some of the cited sources could not have carried a story that old - but the thought of someone causing a riot with a top hat and a jaunty swagger amuses me.

Such remarkable eccentricity should not go unrewarded. It is presumed that Hetherington made a fortune from his sale of such hats, because as we know, top hats became absolutely *the thing* for quite a long time... and hopefully recovered the money in short order.

LUCY HOUSTON (1857-1936)

This one is a bit of a heartbreaker for me. On one hand, she made something possible that resonates with me quite strongly. On the other hand, she was on ideological quicksand, and quite frankly should have known better.

Bar none, the most beautiful thing ever created by Man is the Supermarine Spitfire. It is a marvel of form and function, and the sound of one flying past gives goosebumps to more than one entire generation. It is, quite simply, gorgeous.

And while I say, "created by Man", I should point out that there was one particular Woman without whom none of this would have happened.

After World War One there was very much a feeling among the decision-makers in the British Government that the Royal Air Force was spending far too much time and energy on aircraft development, given that there was no way there was going to be a World War Two.

Supermarine, an aircraft design and manufacture group, were trying to win the Schneider Cup, which was a seaplane race. The Air Ministry vetoed funding, and forbade their pilots from competing in the cup, and forbade RAF aircraft from taking part.

As this was something of a testing bed for aircraft design, it was a bit of a blow, and looked to halt all development on the new Supermarine aircraft... the Spitfire.

The Royal Aero Club - a sporting body in the UK - said that they would try to raise £100,000 (roughly £2 million in today's money) if the government would remove their veto on aircraft and pilots. This was approved mainly because the Air Ministry never thought that the RAC would be able to raise the money in time.

In steps Lady Lucy Houston, born 1857. She famously attacked the stingy Labour Government (who were, admittedly, in the middle of an economic crisis) with the statement:

> *"Every true Briton would rather sell his last shirt than admit that England could not afford to defend herself."*

She donated the entire £100,000 amount herself, allowing Supermarine to not only compete, but win the Schneider Cup with the supremely agile, and outstandingly fast Spitfire float-plane prototype.

After further funding offers were refused by the government, Lady Houston - certainly not shy of blowing her own trumpet - said:

> *"I alone have dared to point out the dire need for air defence of London. You have muzzled others who have deplored this shameful neglect. You have treated my patriotic gesture with a contempt such as no other government would have been guilty of toward a patriot."*

She was loudly, and proudly anti-government, and felt very strongly that the Island Nation would simply not be able to stand up to attack without a strong air force.

In hindsight, she was absolutely correct. However, so far there's no dichotomy. At this point, I'd be simply leaping about shouting "YAY! SPITFIRE!" and doing the happy Spitfire dance.[69]

Alas, it is not all sunglasses and autographs.

Lady Lucy Houston did not consider Germany the threat in the early 1930s. Along with quite a lot of the rest of the world, she saw the rise of Soviet Russia as the burgeoning threat and was convinced that there was a large-scale communist infiltration of Britain.

In fact, she openly admired Germany's leader - a certain Adolf Hitler - for dragging his country out of the economic mess and decay of the First World War and said much the same of Benito Mussolini.

She had a bit of a thing for dictators, you see. She even tried to convince successive British governments to be a bit more like them. She even considered funding the vile Oswald Mosley and his British Union of Fascists... and only decided not to when they (rather short-sightedly) published something unpleasant about her in their newsletter.[70]

So... yay, Spitfires, and boo, Fascists. Mosley, for starters, can eat a large bag of gentleman-sausage... let alone the other two.

I know that a lot of people were quite impressed by the European dictators for their apparent strong leadership, and how they brought their countries kicking and screaming out of the depths of desiccation... so she certainly wasn't alone... but I'm afraid that Lady Houston scores quite highly on my Villainometer for her political views, even if she did help to otherwise help to fund the development of one of my favourite things in the world.

She died in 1936, at the age of 79.

It is unfortunate perhaps that never got to see her legacy in the form of the Spitfire fulfilling its role admirably as the defender of Britain's skies only four years later ... but conversely, she never got to learn just how horrible the political figures she idolised could actually be.

REVEREND W. HOWSE (1820S-1840S)

If you are of a delicate disposition, or if you're eating your breakfast while reading this, I would recommend you gird your loins for a shock to the system... or maybe come back a bit later after your food has had a chance to settle. This one's more than a little bit yuck.

Enon Chapel was built in 1823 in London. It was a bit stinky, having been situated atop a sewer... but this served as camouflage for the particular awfulness that was to follow.

I need to preface this with the following caveat:

Historical accounts differ. While I have found multiple sources which support the below, there are several which also suggest things might have happened quite differently. I encourage folk to do their own research and make up your own mind. If you can stomach it.

Reverend W. Howse, was a man of God (ministers usually are, I suppose), and was somewhat apologetic to his congregation when they complained about the smell inside the chapel.

There was also a horrific rat infestation, and clouds of black flies. People would sometimes gag and choke and have to leave sermons early. I can't imagine it would have been particularly pleasant.

This was partly due to the sewer of course, and the fact that London in the early 1800s was suffering from a significant sewage problem.[71] It is also notable that the only thing between the sewer and the congregation was a vault, or cellar, and a single-ply wooden floor, with gaps in it.

Oh... and lots and lots of rotting corpses. Did I mention that?

You see, it appears Minister Howse had morals that were just as foul as the stench coming up through the floors of the chapel. He had permission to bury *some* bodies (in coffins) under the chapel. That wasn't unusual before the burial reforms brought about by the Burial Act of 1852... but these were neither buried, nor in coffins.

Howse was reportedly charging a mere 15 shillings for burials, and they were all going under the chapel floor. Some reports claim there were over 10,000 bodies packed and piled into the vault under the chapel over a 20-year period...

though realistically the number was likely to be considerably less.

That's a lot of shillings, however you look at it, and Howse would have been making a great deal of money indeed.

Now, there's no way that so many coffins could have fitted into an 18m by 9m space ... so the bodies had been removed from the coffins and just... stacked... and covered in quicklime to hasten their decomposition.

So... human mulch. That's what was under the chapel, and quite a lot of it... masquerading as the noxious odour from the sewers.

There were concerns raised, of course, and an investigation did take place in the early 1840s when the sheer number of internments was noted for such a small chapel. Investigators were physically prevented from entering the vault though, and one judged:

> *Extreme unwillingness, and violence, indeed, of the keeper of Enon Chapel, that there must be a very great body of injurious matter concealed.*
> *- "Health of Towns." Select Committee Report. 1843.*

Now, eventually Howse was caught, and his disgusting practices stopped. I'd have to be honest and say that I have no idea what happened to him at this point, but it's safe to say that he would most-certainly not have got off scot-free for what would have been seen as a quite heinous crime back in the early 1800s.

I mean, it's pretty heinous now... and there have been similar situations reported periodically where - for example - a US crematorium was just dumping bodies in a forest, rather than cremating them... but it would have been particularly heinous in God-fearing 1840s London.

The chapel - no longer being used as a chapel - was eventually purchased by a surgeon by the name of George Walker. He had the remains (described as 'a pyramid of bones, and noisome ichor') removed (at his own expense) to Norwood Cemetery.

Not in individual graves... because the remains were, for the most part, far too far gone for that... but in a single mass-grave around 20 feet deep. For a while, Enon Chapel was rented out to anyone who needed a hall and was not quite so worried about its gruesome history.

A teetotallers society rented the chapel on weekends for three years with the advertising flyer written thus:

> *Enon Chapel - Dancing on the Dead - Admission threepence. No lady or*

gentleman admitted unless wearing shoes and stockings.

... which is ironic, I think, because I feel that you'd probably need a stiff drink.

MIR JAFAR (1691-1765)

Born Syed Mir Jafar Ali Khan Bahadur, his notoriety kicked in in the mind 1750s when he became the symbol of betrayal and treachery for generations to come.

Mir Jafar was a commander in the Bengali army during the rise to prominence of the British East India Company - the powerful mercantile/military organisation that helped build the British Empire.

However you feel about colonialism (let's face it, it is not in vogue at the moment) it is pretty evident that the British East India Company had a reputation for ruthlessness. They very much wanted control of India, and one of the first steps to gain this was military action in Bengal, on the east coast of India.

The problem was that the Bengali forces - and their French allies - outnumbered the British by a considerable margin, and it was unlikely that a British military action would result in much more than an embarrassing defeat for the British.

The British famously do not like defeat. They basically hung their hats on the twin hooks of victory and perseverance, and it was a brave general who would trip off back to blighty with his cap in his hands to let it be known that he had guffed royally and had all their ships sunk.

Enter Mir Jafar, the trusted commander, and a right-hand man to the ruling Nawab of Bengal.

With battle imminent, and the Nawab's court in uproar over what basically amounted to who could grab whatever wealth from the unfolding situation, Mir Jafar and the English commander Robert Clive (aka: Clive of India) made a skullduggerous agreement:

Mir Jafar would support the British forces, and in return, when the British East India Company took over, he would be made Nawab of Bengal, and be given vast wealth.

It was too good to be true. Robert Clive agreed to the betrayal (it was actually quite a complicated arrangement involving two contracts, and multiple parties) and the ball began to roll.

When battle commenced in Plassey, West Bengal, Clive sent his (roughly) 3,000 men into the field against the Nawab's army of over 50,000.

These are odds that would scream "Run away!" at most commanders. It doesn't matter how well-trained your troops are if they only get one or two shots in before over ten times their number descend upon them with sharp objects. The British forces were arrogant, but as a rule, they were not known for stupidity.

As Clive's forces advanced, one whole side of the Nawab's forces - who should have swept down upon them and routed them - refused to join the fight... those men under the command of Mir Jafar.

This was enough. Advancing to key positions and setting up artillery barrages, Clive was able to drive back the rest of the Nawab's splintered army - themselves likely in shock at the unexpected betrayal - and the field was won. After eleven hours of fighting, the British had lost barely 20 men.

And so, Mir Jafar became the new Nawab of Bengal, under the watchful eye of the British East India Company, and Clive of India himself... and the battle proved to be instrumental in enabling the British domination of the entire Indian subcontinent.

The new Nawab of Bengal - formerly Mir Jafar - was now a puppet of the British, and while initially quite pleased with the trappings of power, soon realised that the British wanted more of Bengal than he was willing - or perhaps even able - to provide.

Betrayal being in his nature, Jafar tried to divest himself of his newfound allies by taking up with their deadly rivals, the Dutch East India Company. This would likely have worked quite well for him, had the British not soon thereafter absolutely splattered the Dutch forces in the Battle of Chinsurah.

> *This is where things get a little disjointed and messy... but to summarise...*

Not at all comfortable with Jafar playing both ends against the middle, the British forcibly deposed him, and installed his son, Qasim, as their puppet Nawab. Qasim was rather less smitten by British coin than his father and did his best to drive the British East India Company out of India.

The British weren't having a bar of this because a puppet should puppet. It was absolutely not cricket for a puppet to form strategic alliances and try to force you into the ocean with your tail between your legs.

As colonisers and conquerors, however, the British were very adept, and Qasim was defeated in the Battle of Buxar, and... yep, as such things always rise to the top, Jafar emerged from the undergrowth to once again be crowned as Nawab of Bengal. There he remained until his death, a year later, in 1765.

After his death, the whole region devolved into warring states, each fighting against the other, buying weapons from the British (and French) forces, who were more than happy to support whoever happened to best fit their own interests.

The rest, as they say, is history.

To this day, the word "Mirjafar" is used in Bengal as an epithet, meaning much the same as 'traitor' or 'quisling' does in English. This is the legacy of Jafar, who through avarice changed the history of an entire subcontinent forever.

Mir Jafar would support the British forces, and in return, when the British East India Company took over, he would be made Nawab of Bengal, and be given vast wealth.

KING JOHN (1166-1216)

Formerly Prince John, and all mixed up in the Robin Hood legends, King John (Because he won. Don't let the tales of 'Merry Men' derring-do deceive you.) was every bit as bad as the tales made him out to be.

Prince John became King John upon the death of Richard the Lionheart on a military campaign in France. (In March 1199, Richard died of gangrene after being hit by a crossbow bolt.)

RAISING TAXES

He levied unpopular taxes contrary to customs of the day, and did so outside of military campaigns, which was just unheard of. This made him quite a few enemies.

He brought in a form of inheritance tax, but it was often so steep that the local barons had no hope of paying, with the upshot being that their lands were defaulted to the crown. This made him even more enemies.

He brought in income taxes and taxes against particular religious or ethnic groups. In short, he taxed and taxed until he could tax no more. At one point, his government was hoarding so much silver coinage that whole swathes of the country had to resort to barter, because there wasn't a coin to be found.

THE ARCHBISHOP OF CANTERBURY

The senior bishop of the Church of England is the Archbishop of Canterbury. Appointment of this powerful figure had historically always been a sticking point for English royalty... but in this case King John was very unhappy with the appointment, as he had earmarked one of his lackeys for the role.

When the pope refused to acknowledge John's choice, John took lands belonging to the church and various other possessions. This was viewed as stealing directly from the pocket of the Pope. You did not pilfer from the papacy in medieval times.

He was excommunicated by Rome as a result which was a massive deal back in the 1200s. John was not particularly religious (which itself was scandalous back in the day) but the Pope's subsequent ban on almost all religious observance in England did not sit well with the rest of the population.

King John decided this was a religious declaration of war, and instead of trying to calm things down, started seizing land from the church all over the country. The Pope was absolutely livid, as you can imagine... but excommunication was basically their biggest weapon, and John didn't seem to mind all that much.

Ultimately, however, King John was humiliated by the experience, as the tide of public opinion (remember, religion was the absolute cornerstone of life back in the 1200s) was turning against him. He ended up paying considerable compensation to the papacy and relinquishing much of the stolen land, just to buy back some public support.

THE YOUNG HOSTAGES

The most telling villainy, however, is the tale of the hostages John had taken. In order to keep Welsh Prince Llewellyn in line[72], John had kidnapped 28 children of the Welsh nobility and was holding them in Nottingham Castle.

These were boys, generally between the ages of 12 and 14. The idea being that the Welsh nobility, who obviously wanted their kids back, would put pressure on Llewellyn to remain subservient to the crown.

After some time, news came to the King that Prince Llewellyn had again risen in revolt.

This isn't *really* the case, though Llewellyn was perhaps not as careful as he could have been to avoid raising the King's wrath, but it was enough for John's Machiavellian schemes to foment.

King John rode from his hunting palace in Clipstone and ordered the murder of all of the hostages. The children were all dragged out of the castle and hung from the battlements while King John watched.

He then, according to the tales, declared:

> *"By the teeth of God I will not eat again until I have wreaked my vengeance!"*

... and launched an invasion into Wales.

The invasion was ultimately abandoned when John received threats from other nobles, from England and Scotland alike, greatly angered by his actions.

DEATH AND LEGACY

Naturally, John died while on a military campaign, but not of any heroic derring-do. No, he contracted dysentery in 1216 and shat himself to death. A fitting end, perhaps, to such a villainous monarch.

Throughout history, he was viewed favourably by scholars throughout the Tudor period and beyond, mainly because of his opposition to the papacy, and his promotion of special rights for the monarchy.

From the 19th century onwards however, he was viewed as "almost superhumanly wicked" (Ref: Norgate, 1887) with his cruel personality having been the primary reason for his downfall.

> *Modern scholars tend to view King John as an unsuccessful monarch with dangerous personality traits, though cite that he was an able administrator, and worthy general, for the most part... but still "one of the worst kings ever to rule England"*
> *- Gillingham (2001)*

Either way, his rule can be comfortably encapsulated thusly:

> *The dramatic ambivalence of his personality, the passions that he stirred among his own contemporaries, the very magnitude of his failures, have made him an object of endless fascination to historians and biographers.*
> *- Hollister (1961)*

KING JOHN VI OF PORTUGAL (1767-1826)

A king of Portugal who ordered the creation of many beneficial institutions, scientific, artistic, and judicial in nature - and established education programmes for his people.

The name "King John" tends to be synonymous with villainy, but with this chap, it depends upon who you speak to. Many of his peers thought he was actually a pretty stand-up sort of fellow... but he's come to be ridiculed in later years.

He was (not my words) "subjugated by a shrewish wife" - as his wife, Carlota Joaquina of Spain, would frequently conspire against him in order to promote Spanish interests over those of her adopted Portugal. Not villainous in and of itself.

He is said to have been a "disgusting glutton" who would always keep a baked chicken in his pockets, so that he could snack on them with greasy fingers no matter the time of day. (I find it hard to criticise this. I'm rarely without a Peperami, myself.)

Conversely...

> *If there is agreement among all authors who relied on the testimony of those who knew him closely for his kindness and affability, all the rest is controversy. - Martins, pp 24-25*

Many within his own circle, however, were not happy with his financial aptitude - and certainly he had this tendency to grow his nation's debt, tended to heap titles and privileges on the wealthy, and his government was so full of corruption that you'd be unlikely to get anything done without crossing someone's palm with silver.

The French certainly didn't like him, though the early 1800s were a period in which the French (thanks to a certain Mr Napoleon) were a bit boisterous in general... but they felt John VI was a coward and an aesthete... which... OK? I guess.

All of this could just be passed off as "Well, that's politics, innit?" - and yes, if you look at the world today, there are similarities in some quarters that will be evident to some, if not to others... but villainy?

Frankly, I wouldn't even have considered him

were it not for the relationship between France and Portugal. The relationship being, France wanted Portugal, wouldn't take "Não!" for an answer, and invaded in force in 1807.

There are certain obligations that a monarch has. Foremost being the defence and wellbeing of his people. So, did John VI organise his forces to repel the French invasion? Did he send forth armies of mediators to seek a peaceful solution that everyone could live with? No. He most certainly did not.

Did he mobilise the Portuguese fleet, at least? Well, sort of.

He gathered his family and closest friends together, along with all of their portable wealth, piled everything onto the Portuguese Fleet, and scarpered off to Brazil to leave his people to manage the war all by themselves.

Which they didn't. Quite spectacularly.

The French quickly occupied the entire country and appropriated or disbanded the Portuguese army. They didn't hold it for much more than a year, as there was a popular uprising, but nevertheless, the French had few problems riding into Lisbon because - without its leadership - the Portuguese forces really didn't know what to do. I can only imagine the French general, upon arriving in Lisbon and realising that John

VI and his cronies had fled, snorting through his ridiculous moustache and muttering "Typical" under his breath.[73]

So, what was John's reception in Brazil like, as he hove into view with his entourage and flipping great wodges of cash? Well... he was King of there too... his full title being King of the United Kingdom of Portugal, Brazil and the Algarves... so his reception was pretty good.

When he left Brazil, however, and returned to Portugal, he almost completely emptied Brazil's treasury, and left the country within a hair's breadth of bankruptcy... and was almost certainly a contributing factor in Brazil's later declaration of independence from Portugal.

A further significant blow to the Portuguese economy, because guess where most of their wealth came from? Yeah. Bite the hand that feeds you, and all that.

In March 1826, John VI lunched at the Hieronymites Monastery, and then spent several days feeling quite ill. He died on 9 March, leaving his daughter - the Infanta Isabel Maria - as regent. Poisoning was suspected, but never proven at the time - though later forensic evidence (obtained in 1990) found enough arsenic in his remaining heart fragments to kill two people.

BRINSLEY LE POER TRENCH (1911-1995)

We've had a resurgence of late in people who claim to believe that the Earth is flat, that aliens secretly run the world, and that birds aren't real. There's a lot of conspiracy theorycrafting about, but even though it seems to be picking up... it really isn't anything new.

Even as recently as the 1970s, William Francis Brinsley Le Poer Trench, 8th Earl of Clancarty, and 7th Marquess of Heusden, in the United Kingdom, was convinced that the planet was hollow, and full of flying saucers.

Trench was born to nobility and raised in wealth.[74] He was fairly well educated, and relatively well-liked... but he had a singular mission... to promote the idea that aliens were among us, and that humanity should be made aware.

Through dint of birth, and inheritance of a seat in the British Parliament, in 1975 Trench had the opportunity to leverage his influence to improve the health and wellbeing of the common man, and the infrastructure of Britain.

Instead, he oversaw the introduction of a UFO study group to the House of Lords, and insisted that all information held by the British Government about aliens be made public.

He created quite the furore, ultimately resulting in government officials - from the Lords to the Department of Defence - being forced to declare publicly that they were not holding any information about aliens. A statement at which Trench publicly scoffed.

US President Eisenhower - he claimed - had met five different species of extra-terrestrial in the 1950s, and that they had demonstrated their psychic powers - and powers of invisibility - and the decision had been made to keep the visitations quiet.

Now, I'm not here to cast shade on someone who believes that there is more to the universe than we are necessarily aware. The scientist in me demands, in fact, that consideration be made that everything we know and understand could, quite conceivably, be wrong.

However, I maintain that Trench's aggressive pursuit of 'the truth', whilst flying in the face of overwhelming evidence, and at the detriment of actual commitment to governance, was an excessive extravagance at the height of some quite considerable turmoil and hardship in British society.

Trench remained unconvinced, continued to promote his views about aliens up through government, and devoted significant time and energy to the publicity of his theory that the Earth was hollow.

Not just hollow, but that there were entrances to a vast underground labyrinth at the north and south poles... that the vast caverns had been carved out by Atlanteans... and that icebergs were artificial, because they were composed of fresh water.

The Earth having a molten iron core was - quite frankly - a tissue of lies spread as misinformation to keep people from guessing that it was actually a hollow ball, chock-full of several allied species of very advanced aliens, their inter-dimensional spacecraft, and warm and fruitful oceans.

The fact that each of Trench's assertions could be easily disproved or explained did nothing to convince him that he was in any way incorrect...

but that's a fairly well documented phenomenon among conspiracy theorists in general, I suppose.

He very-much believed that the works by Erich von Däniken (which talked about early human contact with aliens) were true, and furthermore, he (it is claimed) believed that Adam and Eve were not only real people... but were Martians, and that their being 'cast out' of the Garden of Eden was actually representative of their relocation from (the once fertile) Mars, to Earth.

... and this went on for decades. Through the institutional mistrust and crippling inflation of the 1970s, the riots and economic failures of the 1980s, and only really ended with his death in 1995.

Trench was not a *bad* man. He was generally well-liked it seems, and as far as I'm aware he led a largely inoffensive life... but his apparent monomania about UFOs certainly left little room for using his position for... what could comfortably be argued... more beneficial outcomes... and, in my humble opinion, hammers home the dangers of hereditary title in a modern government.

JAMES LIND (1716-1794)

In 18th century, the British Royal Navy was considered one of the strongest military forces on the planet. However, more sailors were killed by disease than enemy action... scurvy being among the most deadly and debilitating diseases facing those on long voyages.

James Lind is credited with performing one of the first ever clinical trials, in his role as surgeon aboard the HMS Salisbury. There were many 'cures' for scurvy, but nobody had looked at efficacy, and sailors were dying in droves.

Naval medicine was dominated by old-wives' tales and remedies which had no scientific basis. Keeping grass and dirt in the mouth was seen as a prevention for scurvy, for example, as it was felt that sailors caught it from being so far from land. Patent cures were sold to the Navy by "Doctors" with no formal training.[75]

Lind took 12 men from HMS Salisbury who were

suffering from scurvy and divided them into six groups of two each. Each group received a different remedy, based on popular knowledge of the time – remedies which were already in use aboard ocean-going navy vessels.

1. A quart of Cider daily
2. 25 drops of elixir of vitriol three times daily
3. Half a pint of seawater a day
4. A nutmeg sized paste of garlic, mustard seed, horse radish, balsam of Peru, and gum myrrh, three times a day
5. Two spoonful's of vinegar daily
6. Two oranges and a lemon a day

By the end of the first week, the group receiving citrus fruit were well enough to help nurse all the others.

IT WAS NOT UNTIL 42 YEARS LATER THAT THE ADMIRALTY ISSUED AN ORDER FOR THE DISTRIBUTION OF LEMON JUICE TO SAILORS.

Historians still debate why they did not act upon Dr Lind's discovery earlier – but it is likely that Lind's lack of a clear conclusion in his writing, and the prevalence of rival 'cures' – played a significant role in this.

Lemon juice became compulsory on ships a year after Lind's death in 1795. Lind is now seen as the father of naval medicine.

Lind never knew why the lemons worked. He didn't need to. He simply gauged the efficacy of each treatment and noted which one had the highest degree of success. What he did not do well was clearly state his conclusions in his work. His clinical trial only accounted for four pages in the middle of his 450-page treatise on scurvy.

ROBERT LISTON (1794-1847)

In the early 1800s, if you had to visit a doctor... or more specifically a surgeon... for a medical procedure, you'd better hope that they were handy with a scalpel... because anaesthetic was not a thing, and it was going to damn well hurt.

Given that antibiotics were also not a thing, and wouldn't be for almost another 100 years, the tiniest of scratches could turn into something awful, with a name like "bubonic gangrenous sepsis of the ganglia" or something, and the next thing you know you've got to have your leg off.

Your best chance of survival was to ensure that your surgeon was pretty good at what he did, and very quick... because the last thing you wanted was someone who was sawing away for half an hour while you were trying to distract yourself by counting screams backwards.

Robert Liston was famous for his speed with the blade. In 1837, he wrote:

> *"Operations must be set about with determination and completed rapidly."*

...but it's entirely possible that he let this get away from him somewhat. It's true that he could remove a limb in less than a minute... but at what cost?

In one surgery, he removed a patient's leg in around 28 seconds. In doing so, he accidentally amputated several of his assistant's fingers. The assistant later died of sepsis. A viewing member of the public was struck by a scalpel during Liston's frenzy - though it did not pierce skin - and died of shock. The patient also died. It must have been an absolute frenzy of surgical body-horror.

In that one operation, Liston had technically lost three people... and only one of them was poorly on the way in!

That's not to say he was a *bad* person in general.

For starters, his overall mortality rate was one death out of every seven amputations. The average at the time was around one in four... so he likely saved more people than he killed.

He was also profoundly ethical in that he stood up for patient's rights, both alive and dead. He was quite famous for removing cadavers that had been ghoulishly displayed for entertainment in order to ensure that the poor people involved had a proper burial. Patient advocates were few and far between in the 19th century.

He would also operate on the poor (who could not afford proper surgery) in the poorest of tenements, to treat those with the greatest need. This earned him the ire of his peers, who felt it beneath the elite profession, and he was banned from several prestigious medical facilities as a result.

I'm not even going to talk about his successful removal (in under five minutes) of a 4.5lb (2kg) scrotal tumour that the poor patient had been carrying around in a wheelbarrow.[76]

But with a cry of "Time me, gentlemen!" he also accidentally cut someone's testicles off when removing their leg as quickly as he could... so "slapdash" was probably right up there as an important word in any lexicon which discussed his professionalism whilst holding a scalpel.

Another rather tragic case saw a boy brought to him with a pulsating lump on his neck. One colleague thought it was a dangerous aneurism of the carotid artery. Liston was sure it was just an abscess. When his colleague urged caution, Liston cried "Oh, poo!" and took a scalpel to it... and the boy died of blood loss within minutes.

Nevertheless, he was made the first Professor of Clinical Surgery at University College Hospital in London in 1835.

Given his extreme unpopularity among his peers, some of the tales attributed to Liston may be apocryphal... but if we take these stories as factual, at least in the major details... then Liston was not the hero of this tale.

He may have had a knack with the blade when it came to quickly removing a limb... and he may have genuinely wanted to help the poor and needy above the wealthy and influential... but a lack of due caution, and any careless death, casts him firmly in the role of villain.

Liston died of an aneurysm in 1847, at the age of 53. Over 500 people - mostly colleagues, friends, and former students - attended his funeral at Highgate Cemetery in London.

VICTOR LUSTIG (1890-1947)

Lustig had the reputation as one of the most notorious con artists of his time, and is infamous for two particularly high-profile cons. The conman's cry of "Would you like to buy a bridge?" had nothing on this chap.

AUSTRIA

Born in 1890 in Austrian-Hungary to a moderately well-off family, Lustig proved to be quite a troublemaker at school. He was a top performing student, but got side-tracked by the high-life, got himself into gambling and womanising, and began a very quick detour towards villainy.

Lustig was fluent in several languages, and was remarkably clever in many ways, and he applied this to his cons. He would often appear to be quite trustworthy and was reportedly quite the charmer when it came to convincing people to part with their money.

His early career was spent on cruise-liners prior to the first world war, and he would approach wealthy tourists to convince them that he was a Broadway producer seeking funds to produce the next big hit.

When the cruise industry was all-but demolished by the outset of war, he moved to USA. His first high-profile con there was to convince a bank to give him money in exchange for property bonds. Using sleight-of-hand and an air of remarkable confidence, he managed to leave the premises with both the cash, and the bonds.

UNITED STATES

One of his most notorious cons was to convince people to buy a device which he said he had invented, which would allow the identical reproduction of any denomination of currency. You feed a note - he said - into one end, wait six hours, and your original note, plus a perfect copy, would come out of the other.

He would wait with his 'mark' to prove that the device worked, and then refuse to sell it to them unless they offered him a particularly high amount. The box - of course - did no such thing and was simply a cunning little repository of notes that would be spat out at six-hourly intervals by clockwork. (Early designs were rather more manual). Upon sale, the purchaser would receive the box, which had been packed with a few notes to give Lustig time to clear the area and escape.

He actually pulled this con on a Texas sheriff and stung him for thousands of dollars. Upon realising that he'd been tricked, the sheriff chased Lustig all the way to Chicago, where he caught up with him. Such was Lustig's way with words that he convinced the sheriff that he simply wasn't using the device properly. As a show of good faith, however, Lustig returned his money. It wasn't until some hours after Lustig left that the sheriff realised that the money was counterfeit, and Lustig had defeated him yet again.

After the war, Lustig returned to France, and keeping with his usual form, decided to make himself a bit of money.

FRANCE

Noticing an article in the local paper about how much money it was costing the French government to maintain the Eifel Tower, Lustig had some government letterhead forged for him. He sent invitations out to scrap metal dealers and offered them a chance to capitalise on the removal and melting down of the Eifel Tower... something that could prove to be spectacularly lucrative.

He selected André Poisson - the owner of such a business - as a likely mark, and then approached him to say that he would be awarded the contract... but only if he paid a bribe to Lustig. Poisson was a bit of a social climber, so he readily agreed, and Lustig fled to Austria with 70,000 francs... well over a million US dollars in today's money.

Hiding out in Austria, Lustig was rather surprised to find that the news of the scam had not hit the papers. He checked for months, before deciding that Poisson had been too embarrassed by falling for the scam and had not gone to the authorities. He was right.

So, later in the year, Lustig returned to Paris, and sold the Eifel Tower again. The mark this time was not too embarrassed, and Lustig ended up having to flee to America to avoid arrest.

BACK IN THE UNITED STATES

One of his most dangerous ploys was a con he ran on none other than Al Capone himself - the notorious Depression-era gangster. The economy in USA in the 1930s had tanked, so it would have taken quite a lot of effort for Lustig to convince Capone to give him $50,000 for a scam... and yet he did.

However, it was a little more complicated than that. He kept the money in a safety deposit box in a bank, and then returned it to Capone two months later stating that the scam had fallen through. This impressed Capone, who decided that Lustig was an honest man, and he was subsequently convinced to loan the conman $5,000 to 'tide him over' until another opportunity presented itself.

Lustig then took this money, and invested it in a large-scale, and very lucrative, counterfeiting operation. This drew the attention of the Federal Authorities, but with careful planning, Lustig had hidden his steps well.

His failing was with women. He had been cheating on his girlfriend at the time, and when the young lady 'Billy-May' found out about the other woman, she tipped off the authorities, and Lustig was arrested. The day before his trial, he escaped custody due to feigning illness, and using a specially constructed rope ladder. He was on the run for almost a month before being recaptured.

Lustig spent 15 years in prison for his counterfeiting crimes and served them all on Alcatraz. An additional five years was added for his escape.

The conman never saw freedom again. In 1947 Lustig contracted Pneumonia and died in a hospital for federal prisoners, with only two years left on his sentence. His death certificate listed his occupation as "apprentice salesman".

NICCOLÒ MACHIAVELLI (1469-1527)

It would be best to be both loved and feared. But since the two rarely come together, anyone compelled to choose will find greater security in being feared than in being loved.
- Machiavelli

From someone who is a proud political mover and shaker, this is not the sort of thing that you really want to hear. Machiavelli was a diplomat and politician in Italy, and he literally wrote the manual to being a successful amoral dictator.

In fact, in Machiavelli's mind, amoral was the only way to be if you were a leader. If you've got power, he reasoned, you should be prepared to do anything to keep it.

Machiavelli started off life as the third child to

an attorney[77] in Florence, Italy - quite well off in Italian society at the time, though not hugely wealthy. He was very well educated.

Throughout much of Machiavelli's early life, Florence was ruled by the Medici family. Italy was more of a nation of city states than a unified whole, and the Medici were supremely powerful. However, a surge of republican fervour, and an untimely death, resulted in the Medici being expelled from Florence. During this republican period, Machiavelli obtained a post as the producer of government documents, and later became a diplomat.

This exposed him to the machinations of those in power, and he soaked up every tidbit of information that he could find. The brutal methods of *Cesare Borgia*, an Italian cardinal out to build his own little powerbase, for example, were fascinating.

Machiavelli pushed Florence to adopt a citizen-based standing army, rather than hiring mercenaries, as was vogue at the time. Using this, he won several critical battles, though he did lose dramatically to the Spanish as well.

His political influence in Florence was nevertheless growing. One could perhaps say (with a cheeky 'dad joke' snerkle!) that the number one hit in Italy at the time was 'Florence and the Machinations'.

Unfortunately, the military loss left Florence open to Spanish invasion, and the Spanish stormed into the city in 1512, with the Medici hot on their heels and ready to reclaim their power base. Which they did, arresting Machiavelli and torturing him for weeks as a conspirator against the Medici family.

It wasn't just Machiavelli in their sights of course... the Medici were back, and they were ready to party. Most of their furious post-reclamation activity was just to convince Johnny Public that they were back in the big-boy seat, and everyone had better be on their best behaviour.

After his release, Machiavelli retired to the countryside and began to write. This is when he wrote *The Prince*, the work for which he is best remembered.

In this, he urges prospective leaders to eschew the bonds of emotion and theology, and rule with an iron grip. Fear above all else and forget emotion. Murder if you have to.

> *One can say this in general of men: they are ungrateful, disloyal, insincere and deceitful, timid of danger and avid of profit.... Love is a bond of obligation which these miserable creatures break whenever it suits them*

> *to do so; but fear holds them fast by a dread of punishment that never passes. - Machiavelli "The Prince"*

His was a political philosophy rooted in how men behave, not how men should behave, and contains no higher aspiration for improving One's lot beyond the acquisition and retention of power.

Machiavelli wrote of the virtues of the totalitarian ideal, and it became a work much loved by Napoleon and Mussolini, among others.

> *So far as he is able, a prince should stick to the path of good but, if the necessity arises, he should know how to follow evil. - Machiavelli "The Prince"*

The work (and Niccolò Machiavelli himself) has of course been much criticised for this type of outlook - though several noted scholars have stated that it is, perhaps, more of a warning to everyone else about the type of person who tends to gravitate towards power... and perhaps even a work of dark satire.

Machiavelli was a republican to his core. He chafed under the rule of the Medici, and supported the republican leaders that came after, even if he openly deplored their tolerance and kow-towing to religious idealism.

Even today, the word "Machiavellian" refers to unscrupulous acts of political skullduggery, conniving and twisting, and devoid of compassion and empathy. A fitting legacy, perhaps.

In 1527 he died after taking 'a medicine' - suggesting that he may have been poisoned. He left his family in poverty - according to his son at least - while *The Prince* went on to become one of the most famous books ever written.

MARY MALLON (1869-1938)

Lots of people have heard of Typhoid Mary as a sort of mythological figure who spread disease (typhoid, if the name is anything to go by) wherever she went... but it's surprising how many people don't realise that she was a very real person, and that she lived quite recently, in the grand scheme of things.

THE DISEASE

Typhoid is basically salmonella poisoning. Typhoid fever is the fever which accompanies infection. You get it from eating infected food or drinking infected water, and infection can pass from human to human, or human to food to human, etc. A water supply can be infected, which can result in a horribly quick spread of the illness.

There's now a vaccine for typhoid, and a range of antibiotics... but back in the mid-1800s and early-1900s, your options were very limited. Typhoid was a killer back then.

MARY'S EARLY DAYS

Born Mary Mallon in what is now Northern Ireland in 1869, Mary was likely infected with typhoid from birth, as her mother was recorded as having had it during pregnancy.

Demonstrating an aptitude for cooking, Mary emigrated to the United States at the age of 15, and began working as a cook for some fairly well-to-do families of the day. This is where the recorded problems began.

SIGNS OF INFECTION

In 1900-1907, Mary worked for eight families in the New York City area, and seven of these families contracted typhoid. From employers, residents, staff... people were contracting the disease in droves around her. She remained fit and well.

As she moved from home to home, and people began to fall sick in each one... several dying... a sanitation engineer was hired as an investigator to determine where the infection was coming from... Mr *George Soper*.

The investigation into the unanticipated outbreak of typhoid identified Mary as a likely source. Soper - perhaps without a required level of diplomacy - confronted her and demanded a urine and stool sample.

Mary took up a 'carving fork' and chased him

from the property.

Now, to be perfectly honest, if Mary hadn't put two and two together at this point, and was just going about her business, having a strange man come barrelling up to you and demanding you wee into a cup would ring alarm bells for me as well. I might not resort to a carving fork, but I would certainly be sending him away with a flea in his ear. He might get a stool sample, but it would be flung at him as he retreated.[78]

In all fairness to Mary, the concept of an asymptomatic carrier was unknown at the time. It was thought that if you had the disease, then you would suffer the effects of the disease, not just spread it quietly while feeling perfectly well yourself.

THE FIRST QUARANTINE

Mary continued to be unhelpful, even when confronted by the authorities, and in the end, she had to be restrained by five police officers and taken to an isolated facility.

She was found to be absolutely *infested* with typhoid. She admitted to almost never washing her hands. Now in enforced quarantine, she refused to admit that she might be the cause of the illness among those around her, refused to believe that she had typhoid, and refused treatment.

She also declared that she would absolutely continue to work as a cook, because the money was good.

She was in isolation for almost three years, before being released on the understanding that she would cease to work as a cook and would take all steps she could to ensure that she did not spread the disease.

In 1910 she declared she was:

"Prepared to change her occupation and would give assurance by affidavit that she would upon her release take such hygienic precautions as would protect those with whom she came in contact, from infection."

RETURN TO THE COMMUNITY

After a brief stint working as a laundress, paying less than cook, Mary took several fake surnames, and once again took a number of roles working as a cook.

Everywhere she cooked, people became ill with typhoid. Over and over, she would turn up in a job as a cook, infect a family or community, and then change her name and acquire a new job as a cook somewhere else.

She worked in a few kitchens in restaurants, hotels, and spa centers. Almost everywhere she worked, there were outbreaks of typhoid. She was changing jobs so quickly that even following the trail of infection, the ever-vigilant Soper was unable to locate her.

Eventually, she got a job in a hospital, and infected 25 people, two of whom died. Soper was called in to investigate, and recognised Mary's description and handwriting.

SECOND QUARANTINE AND DEATH

After a manhunt, she was located (delivering food to a friend) and arrested and returned to quarantine in 1915.

She spent the rest of her life in quarantine. She was given a small cottage on a quarantine island and allowed supervised trips to the mainland... as well as a job for staff on the island... but she was never again allowed into the general community un-supervised.

Then, in 1938, at age 69, Mary contracted pneumonia and died.

LEGACY AND AFTERMATH

Research by a reliable source led to an estimate that Mallon had contaminated "at least one hundred and twenty-two people, including five dead" - however, because she pointedly refused to cooperate, the full extent of infection was never fully known. Some of the more extreme estimates even put the number of dead at over fifty, and the infected in the high hundreds.

The history of Mary Mallon, declared

"unclean" like a leper, may give us some moral lessons on how to protect the ill and how we can be protected from illness...By the time she died New York health officials had identified more than 400 other healthy carriers of Salmonella typhi, but no one else was forcibly confined or victimized as an "unwanted ill".
- Annals of Gastroenterology (2013)

Mary was absolutely not the only super-spreader of typhoid. There was an outbreak linked to milkmen in various communities - including Boston where there were several... the trail of infection following the route of the milkmen who were either infected themselves or had watered down their product with infected water.

Mary was no-doubt treated poorly and left with little support in a community with few safety nets to stop people from slipping into poverty... but she did continue to work as a cook in defiance of all reason, watching people get sick and die around her as she moved from job to job.

THOMAS MIDGLEY, JR (1889-1944)

Midgley has been described as having a greater impact on Earth's environment than any other single entity, ever. It's a well-deserved label, and a very negative impact, as you will likely see.

Born in 1889, Midgley became a mechanical and chemical engineer. He was an inventor, from a family of inventors.

PETROL LEAD

In 1916, he started working for General Motors.

One of the big problems that the engineers were experiencing was the 'knocking' of the engine - where uncontrolled combustion would cause the engine to run inefficiently and shorten its life - and Midgley took it upon himself to develop a 'cure'.

Which he did, with the addition of Tetraethyl Lead (TEL) to the gasoline mixture. It prevented knocking quite effectively, and Midgley won an award from the American Chemical Society. General Motors seriously downplayed the use of lead in the mix, calling the additive simply 'ethyl'.

It wasn't too long before US Public Health Service warned of the dangers of lead production and leaded fuel. However, these warnings went unheeded. There was simply too much money at stake.

Midgley countered safety concerns with a press conference to demonstrate the apparent safety of TEL. He poured TEL over his hands, placed a bottle of the chemical under his nose, and inhaled its vapor, and said he could do this every day without succumbing to any problems.

> *"Can you imagine how much money we're going to make with this? We're going to make 200 million dollars, maybe even more," said Thomas Midgley, during a phone conversation with Charles Kettering in 1923, while he was recovering from lead poisoning after demonstrating it was totally safe by inhuling leaded gas.*
> *- Interesting Engineering (2018)*

The plant producing the TEL fuel additive was plagued with problems... including cases of lead poisoning, hallucinations, insanity, and five deaths. There were even links found between pre-school lead poisoning levels and violent crime, general health, and neurological impairment, throughout history.

In the US alone, it took nearly 60 years for leaded fuel to be phased out, and in Europe it wasn't until much later. It is estimated that 7 million tons of lead were released into the atmosphere from gasoline in the United States alone. In 2011, a study backed by the United Nations estimated that the removal of TEL had resulted in $2.4 trillion in annual benefits, and 1.2 million fewer premature deaths.

FREON GAS

In the 1920s, if you wanted a refrigerator, you were playing fast and loose with some pretty dangerous materials. The gases used in the refrigeration process were toxic and highly reactive.

Midgley developed the first chlorofluorocarbon (CFC), specifically the rather intense sounding dichlorodifluoromethane, which they marketed as Freon. It revolutionised refrigeration... as you can imagine.

To demonstrate the CFC gas was safe he inhaled a large amount of the gas and blew out a candle flame to show it was non-toxic and non-flammable, therefore, safe.

Midgley won a medal from The Society of Chemical Industry... and CFCs soon took over as the refrigerant of choice... as well as inclusion in aerosols as a propellant.

Safe it was not.

In fact, one kilogram of CFC refrigerants has the same greenhouse impact as two tonnes of carbon dioxide, which is the equivalent of running your car for six months.

Freon (and related CFCs) were one of the primary causes of ozone layer depletion globally. This resulted in more solar radiation penetrating Earth's atmosphere, resulting in shorter sunburn times, and greater risk of skin cancers and eye damage... among other things.

In 1990, more than 90 governments met in London and agreed on a treaty to phase out the ozone-destroying CFC's, by the end of the century. The environmental costs, and the costs to industry, are huge, complicated, and largely incalculable on a global scale.

MIDGLEY'S END

In 1940, at the age of 51, Midgley contracted Polio. This left him largely paralysed. He invented a contraption - a complex system of levers and pulleys - to help him get in and out of bed without any help.

As with Midgley's other inventions, this one came

with a horrific and deadly side effect. In 1944, at the age of 55, Midgley became entangled in his machine, and it strangled him.

I am certainly not one to wish ill on another person... but at this point, it is reasonable to suggest that Thomas Midgley Jr. had contributed to damaging the world more than any other human being.

Noted author Bill Bryson described him as having:

> *"An instinct for the regrettable that was almost uncanny."*

Not all the fallout was Midgley's doing, and he did not necessarily know how far and wide his inventions would spread, or even understand the impact that this would have on a global ecosystem ... but he did clearly and pointedly demonstrate a distinct willingness to deny the risks, all for self-gain.

CHARLES VANCE MILLAR (1854-1926)

Charles Vance Millar was a Canadian lawyer and financier. His life was one of money and influence, but while he had friends, he had no particular family, and had a little bit of a twist to his personality.

Millar lived a fairly successful life. He owned strong companies, and racehorses were his passion. He held the contract for the Canadian mail service, and so forth. In brief, he was not going to be short a bob or two.[79]

Millar was a fairly standard wealthy man in life. In truth, it was really only after his demise that he became something of the a light-hearted prankster ... but he failed, perhaps, to appreciate the impact he was to have in death.

Millar died in his law office in 1926, of a stroke. He collapsed in front of a client and was dead before a doctor could arrive. He was quite well-liked, and many from his profession attended his funeral. His surviving assets were worth somewhere in the region of US$4 million in 1926 - some US $58.2 million in today's money.

Now, when compared to some of the wealthy folk we've mentioned in the book so far, that's not a monster sum... but it was more than enough to set off a chain of events that would have long-lasting repercussions indeed.

Millar was a prankster and knew he would die without heirs... so he wrote a will which tipped parts of Canada on its head. Millar's pranks frequently played on people's greed and forced them to confront their own hypocrisy.

> *This Will is necessarily uncommon and capricious because I have no dependents or near relations and no duty rests upon me to leave any property at my death and what I do leave is proof of my folly in gathering and retaining more than I required in my lifetime.*
> *- Charles Millar's Will (1926)*

The will had four key points, as follows:

The Jamaica Property

Three of Millar's colleagues, with whom he got on quite well, but who he knew utterly despised each other, were granted lifetime tenancy in Millar's vacation home in Jamaica. This would have been seen at the time as a *supremely* desirable property. The catch was the condition that all three men would have to live there together in each other's company.

The Shares in a Brewery

Every practicing Protestant minister in Toronto (at the time famous for their firm stance against alcohol) was given shares in O'Keefe Brewery stock - which was a Catholic business - which only paid out if they were involved in its management and drew upon its dividends.

Shares in Horse Racing Related Business

Two anti-horse-racing advocates who had been quite vocal opponents to Millar's racing, and the industry in general, were gifted shares of Ontario Jockey Club stock, on the understanding that they were shareholders for three years.

Ordained Christian ministers in Walkerville, Sandwich (who were notorious for their anti-horse-racing stance at the time) were each gifted a very valuable share of Kenilworth Park racetrack, in Ontario... with the notable exception of "Spracklin... who shot a hotelkeeper."

All of these could be taken with a little glimmer of puckish delight, because - let's face it - who doesn't like a smug little "how willing are you to compromise your principles for personal gain" prank or two. The final big-ticket item on Millar's will, however...

The Great Stork Derby

Millar's will decreed that the remainder of his estate - which came to a considerable sum - would be converted to cash in 1936 (ten years after his death) and awarded to the Toronto woman who gave birth to the most children in that time. In the event of a tie, the sum would be split evenly.

The will was examined very thoroughly to see if this clause could be declared invalid... it seems some very distant relatives of Millar - who had nothing to do with him at all during his life - had come to light and wanted the money.

Millar, however, was a very good lawyer, and legally the whole thing was airtight. The will survived ten years of litigation and was worth half a million Canadian dollars in 1936... millions in today's money.

The courts did state, however, that children born out of wedlock would not count towards the total - this being 1926 after all.

The derby was widely criticised as a morally dubious affair, especially among the religious community who were - by and large - aghast at Millar's plans. The premier of Ontario province at the time described the derby as:

"The most revolting and disgusting exhibition ever put on in a civilised country."

The thing is - while Millar's plan may have really thrown the cat among the pigeons and encouraged baby-having far beyond the means of some families who were hopeful of winning vast sums of money - there may have been some method to his madness.

Some claim that his plan was perhaps to cast doubt on the wisdom of vocal opponents to birth control in Canada in the 1920s, others claim that it was to set and test certain legal precedents... either (or both) of which could genuinely be true.

However you look at it, the results were eye-watering.

Four women were finally deemed to have won the derby, having given birth to nine children each within the ten-year period.

Annie Katherine Smith, Kathleen Ellen Nagle, Lucy Alice Timleck, and Isabel Mary Maclean - each of whom was given CA$110,000 - worth roughly US$1.8 million in today's money.

While Millar died childless, he could be

considered to have been responsible for the birth of 36 children - all of which had enough money to be very well cared for by 1936 standards - among the winners alone, and goodness knows how many others who did not win, and therefore gained no financial benefit.

MUHAMMAD II OF KHWARAZM (1169-1220)

This tale is perhaps mainly about one man's inability to read the room. When someone who has conquered a good portion of the known world knocks on your door and asks for a cup of sugar, you don't punch him in the face and steal his cup.

Ala ad-Din Muhammad II was the Shah (basically an emperor) of the *Khwarazmian Empire*, which was a region covering parts of central Asia, and what we now call Afghanistan and Iran. It was, at the time, one of the largest empires in the world by surface area - covering an estimated 2.3 million square kilometres.

Muhammad II's reign was expansionist, and successful. He conquered neighbouring states and incorporated them into the empire. His people were actually fairly prosperous when compared to many other nations, and he wasn't unpopular in his core states.

... as far as tyrants go, that is.

The outlying areas he conquered, however, were less enthralled by him, and his reign was fairly brutal if pushed.

For example, in the city of Samarkand, in what is now known as Uzbekistan. After it was conquered by the Khwarazmian Empire around 1207 AD (after a fairly turbulent recent history) the population rebelled against Muhammad II, resulting in the death of many Khwarazmian people. Muhammad II sacked the city and executed somewhere in the region of 10,000 Samarkand citizens.

Force, it seems, was the preferred method for keeping the empire in line, and it worked very well... right up until the neighbours came knocking.

Let's talk briefly about *Genghis Khan*. It's a name that has lasted quite well through history, and there's a reason for that. Genghis Khan and his Mongol armies had swept across two-thirds of what would one day come to be known as China. He was a big fish in an increasingly small pond.

Thing is, he wasn't particularly interested in heading too much further south than he already was... though he certainly wanted to expand further west (and later did) and grow his empire significantly.

What he did want was trading partners. His imperial footprint was huge, but his infrastructure was lacking, so forming relationships with those areas outside of his domain was actually fairly important to his empire.

He sent a small trading delegation to the Khwarazm borders. How many is unclear. Some records say around 100 merchants and dignitaries, with their guards. Others say around 400. Muhammad II had them all arrested, choosing to believe that they were a raiding force. He took all of the trading goods for himself.

In an act of fairly great restraint, I feel, Genghis[80] sent a small delegation of dignitaries to see Muhammad II, and explain that there had been some kind of misunderstanding. Muhammad II had them executed. Doubling down, he also had all of the captured merchants and dignitaries from the previous delegation executed.

Genghis was obviously displeased.[81]

He responded in a slightly less diplomatic manner and decided to express his mild dissatisfaction with the careful application of 150,000 soldiers - who scooted casually across the Khwarazmian border and said - more or less - "All of this is ours now. Where's your boss? We'd like a word."

When no answer was forthcoming, they sacked the cities of Samarkand[82], Bukhara, Otrar, and the capital city of Urgench.

Muhammad II in the meantime had run away, rather than face the wrath of Genghis, who was notoriously inventive when it came to discussing his dissatisfaction with those who had directly offended him.

Only a few weeks later, Muhammad II died of pleurisy on a small island in the Caspian Sea, his empire - and reputation - in tatters. Perhaps he should have handed over that cup of sugar after all.

REMARKABLE PEOPLE

Force, it seems, was the preferred method for keeping the empire in line, and it worked very well... right up until the neighbours came knocking.

JOHN MYTTON (1796-1834)

Born into privilege in 1796, John "Mad Jack" Mytton was destined to be spoiled. He grew up in Shropshire, not far from the Welsh border in England, to be a notorious drunk, an honest-to-goodness 'eccentric', and one of the most outwardly corrupt politicians ever to be elected.

In the 18th and 19th centuries in Britain, money spoke volumes. You might be forgiven for thinking that it still does... because let's face it... it does... but back in the early 1800s you could buy just about anything.

Mytton received an annual income of around £10,000, which might not sound like a great deal if you're used to today's values ... but back around 1800, the average annual income of a labourer was around £12, and a bailiff would be paid around £20 a year... so £10,000 a year was a lot of money by anyone's estimation.

EARLY YEARS AND EDUCATION

Mytton's wealth and position had him buy a spot in the prestigious Westminster School, London. He wasn't there long, however, as he picked a fight with a teacher over some inconsequentiality or other and was expelled under something of a cloud.

This didn't stop him academically. He was also given a spot in Trinity College, Cambridge. He attended at age 20, and it is said that he took with him some 200 bottles of port to sustain himself through his studies. Needless to say, he didn't get a lot of studying done, and was never awarded a degree.

I mean, you're never going to turn up to anywhere with 200 bottles of port and get a lot of work done, are you? This is all irresponsible, but hardly *particularly* remarkable so far... unless you count the incredible wasted opportunity. I sort-of do. Back in the 1800s, many people would have killed for the chance to attend such a prestigious school, and Mytton basically pissed on it because he was bored.

MILITARY CAREER

It wasn't just education that was up for sale in the 1800s. You could actually buy a military rank. The thinking being that the wealthy landed gentry would be natural leaders, and if you could afford to be a captain in the cavalry, then you'd automatically be good at it.[83]

With this type of thinking it actually amazes me that England became such a global superpower. There are so many stories of fools with money who purchased their rank and got so many of their troops killed.

Mytton became a captain in the Yeomanry Cavalry. He later became a Cornet (second lieutenant) in the 7th Hussars. This was during the Peninsula Wars against Napoleon... and Mytton spent his time gambling and carousing. Upon returning to England, he was conferred the rank of major. Because nothing says 'distinguished military career' like rolling dice, playing cards, and drinking port.

HUNTING PROWESS

One can't be a squire in the early 1800s and not have a healthy regard for the noble sport of hunting, can One? Mytton liked the foxes. Or rather, he so vehemently didn't like the foxes that he had a large pack of hounds of his own and used to run them at every possible opportunity.

At one point he was believed to own somewhere in excess of 2,000 dogs. How many of these were hunting dogs is not recorded.

Furthermore... he had something of a penchant for hunting in the nude and would frequently strip completely naked and - atop horse - continue the hunt *au naturel*.[84]

His horse, Baronet, was such pride and joy to him that it used to have free run of his home, and the two could often be found sitting by the fire in the main hall enjoying the warmth.

OTHER ODDITIES

For someone who liked to hunt starkers, his wardrobe consisted of 150 pairs of hunting breeches, 700 pairs of handmade hunting boots, 1,000 hats and some 3,000 shirts.

- He used to equip his stable boys with ice-skates and have them chase rats.
- Once, in order to cure his hiccups, he set fire to his own nightgown with a candle. This worked.
- He tried to jump over a toll-bridge with a horse-and cart. This did not work.

POLITICAL HEAVYWEIGHT

So, here's the kicker. At age 23, Mytton decided he would quite like to be a politician... specifically a Tory MP... so decided to run for election in Shrewsbury.

You'd think that being quite the lad-about-town, he might be pretty popular, and be able to swing quite a few votes his way by sheer force of personality... but why chance your burgeoning political career on the vagaries of some serf's political leanings, right?

Instead, he offered people £10 per vote. Bear in

mind that this is a world where a labourer would be paid £12 per year... so we're not talking a small amount of money here. He threw tens of thousands of dollars at acquiring enough votes to land him the job as Member of Parliament for Shrewsbury... and he loved it. His political rivals loved it less and declared that he had stolen the seat by 'pecunious means'... but money talks, and their declarations fell upon deaf ears.

They needn't have worried too much, however. Attending his first debate at the House of Commons, Mytton was bored within 30 minutes, and never set foot in the place again. He did not stand for re-election and gave the whole thing up as a bad lark.

DECLINE AND DEATH

Wine, women, and amateur dramatics were starting to get the better of him, and years of unsound financial decisions were finally taking their toll. (He had been married, but his wife had run away.)

Mytton was in debt, He was told by his accountant that if he were but to live on £6,000 of his annual £10,000 income, his debts would be paid quickly, and no assets would have to be sold. He scoffed, and famously shouted:

> *"I wouldn't give a damn to live on £6,000 a year!"*

... again, in a world where a bailiff – considered quite well-paid – would earn £20 a year.

He fled to France to avoid his creditors, with an attractive young lady who he had met on a bridge and offered £500 a year to become his... erm... special friend.[85] He wasn't there for long and returned to England after he thought the fuss might have died down a bit. It had not, and he was imprisoned in King's Bench Prison in Southwark for debts unpaid.

He died there, age 37, described as a "round-shouldered, tottering, old-young man bloated by drink, worn out by too much foolishness, too much wretchedness and too much brandy."[86]

Some might argue he was simply a young fool who became too wealthy too early, and there'd be a good deal of truth in that... but a feckless life lived frivolously, wasting all the advantages that so many others would have been desperate for, is pretty villainous in my book.

ORESTES (AROUND 450AD)

While I certainly wouldn't call The Romans 'goodies', they are not the focus of this story, so much as one general who took the teetering empire up to the edge of the cliff, and gave it a damn good shove.

The Roman empire was big even by today's standards, covering quite a lot of the known world, and bringing with it technology and systems of governance that would last for hundreds of years. When it fell, however, it fell hard.

Orestes was born into aristocracy in the Western Roman Empire, and lived a life of privilege and influence. He fancied himself as a political leader and warrior, and in 475 AD was appointed magister militum (A high level strategic commander) by Western Roman Emperor Julius

Nepos.

In the grand scheme of things, this was probably not a great idea... but the belief that being born into aristocracy granted one certain abilities was still alive and well. Rome was not really a meritocracy.

It was also not a great idea because one of the first things that Orestes did, when he had control of military forces, was depose Julius Nepos, and take over... making his 12-year-old son Emperor, in a sort-of "It doesn't look as bad as me being in charge... but I'm still actually in charge" kind-of way.

The rest of Rome wasn't too thrilled about this... but given that the two Eastern Roman Emperors were actually at war with each other, they couldn't really take time out of their busy schedules to stomp the uppity newcomer.

Not that they had to.

You see, in order to depose Nepos, Orestes had employed mercenaries. This was perfectly normal at the time. Most of the Roman army was mercenary in nature, and as long as you paid them, they'd be fine. Thing is... Orestes had promised to pay them in land, in Northern Italy. Politically, however, this would have been a remarkably hard sell, so instead of paying them in land, Orestes decided to... well... not.

You can imagine that this went down like a kitten-burger at a vegan barbeque, and the mercenaries, under their commander Odoacer gathered his men and decided to take the promised land by force. They raided every town and village in Northern Italy, and because almost all of the troops who were guarding these areas were the self-same mercenaries, they met very little resistance.

Having completed this, they looked around and thought... why stop here?

Orestes of course, had practically no military experience. He relied on his mercenary commanders who, at this point, were treating Northern Italy like a fox treats a henhouse. He gathered what non-mercenary troops were available - which were precious few - and hid behind the walls of the fortress-city of Pavia, and the protection of its bishop.

The Mercenaries shrugged, kicked down the walls, ransacked the place, and chased Orestes and his men across Italy.[87]

Orestes, with an overconfidence likely often felt by the incompetent, decided he had the military advantage, and met them in the field for a decisive final battle.

While his troops were crack troops, certainly, the mercenaries were no slouches either, and they had the advantage of numbers and experienced leadership. Orestes and his men were quickly overwhelmed... and Orestes himself was executed.

Rome had certainly had its ups and downs by the 5th century, and was a shadow of its former self - fractured and ripe for collapse. The fact that a band of largely foreign mercenaries was able to overthrow so much of it certainly put one of the few remaining nails in its coffin... and Rome, such as it was by the stage... fell into ruin.

Oh, not overnight, to be sure... but Odoacer's defeat of Orestes is seen as deeply influential, and a clear indicator that Rome was no longer able to enforce its rule... and it was only a matter of time before the wolves at the gate started to dig.

JOHN OVERS (EARLY 1100S)

There's a terrifying tale of the afterlife in which The Ferryman, Charon, a skeletal horror, ferries the dead across the river Styx... assuming you have placed coins upon the closed eyes of the departed.

Well... the ferryman in this particular tale was called John Overs, and he used to ferry anyone across the Thames if they had a coin or two... and it turns out he was a bit of a plonker. Oh, we're not talking recent history either, so this tale is likely apocryphal, at least in the detail... we're looking at the period of around 1120 AD, some 900 (and change) years ago.

In the years before there were bridges crossing the Thames, the ferryman was an important and quite well-paid role, particularly if you had a half-way decent ferry-boat, and could take across a carriage.

John Overs was wealthy. He had enough land

for a dock at each side of the river, servants, crew, a daughter on the cusp of marriage, and... unfortunately a rather miserly streak. His penny-pinching ways put him at odds with many of his staff. He would clip their earnings at the merest opportunity, skimped on safety, and was forever concocting elaborate schemes to get out of paying for this or that expense.

One day, he decided that - should he die - his staff would go on a period of mourning... and mourning meant fasting. This would, he calculated, save him a full day's provisions... so he faked his death in bed.

Upon finding him 'deceased' however, his staff did not go into a period of mourning. They celebrated by cracking open his finest victuals and had quite the 'wake' in his 'honour'. Quite incensed that his plan had backfired, and that this was going to cost him quite a bit of money, Overs got angrily out of bed and charged downstairs to confront the wayward servants.

One of them, seeing his deceased boss re-animated (and in something of a fit of 'this is costing me money' rage), clouted him with an oar, believing the devil had taken possession of the corpse. The blow, alas, actually did kill the ferryman.

Mary, who was the daughter of Overs, had by

this stage already sent word to her fiancé that her father was deceased, and he had acquired a horse and was galloping to claim both her and her father's inheritance. Alas, he fell from his horse and snapped his neck, rendering him also stone dead.

Mary, it is said, in her grief founded a convent and became a nun. This convent, by accounts, later became part of The Cathedral and Collegiate Church of St Saviour and St Mary Overie, right by south bank of what in later years became London bridge.

The dock, on the other hand, is today the berth of the *Golden Hinde II*, a rather fine, and quite seaworthy, replica of the flagship with which famed explorer Sir Francis Drake circled the globe, between 1577 and 1580.

ROBERT PEARY (1856-1920)

American explorer, and naval officer, Peary is best known for leading an expedition that claimed to be the first to have reached the geographic North Pole, in 1909.

Explorers tend to be a hardy lot. They can put up with privations and hardships that most of us would freak out at... like a literal wasteland of frozen ocean, or cold so intense that it would snap your tonker off if you weren't careful enough having a whiz.

I for one would rather avoid this, so my exploration tends to occur in places where One can whiz with wild abandon, without fear of meteorological reprisal.

Peary cared not a jot, for he was a rugged polar bear of a man... and in April 1909 the Pole was within his reach. He and another explorer called Matthew Henson beetled about (separately) quite close to the top of the world, and Peary stated he was quite certain that in his ambling he had crossed the pole.

Henson, who was the most qualified to measure the pole's location, stated that it was him, and that he was the first man who had ever actually sat on the top of the world... much to Peary's disgruntlement.

When they both returned to civilisation, the powers that be decided that Peary was the Northernmost explorer. Peary had actually lobbied to get his claim recognised over that of Henson, even though it was clear from the outset that Henson was the most likely candidate.[88]

It wasn't until a full review in 1988 that the decision was reversed, given that Henson's notes were far clearer than Peary's, that Peary's timings didn't add up, and a few other inconsistencies ... and it is believed that Henson got to the actual pole, while Peary had just ambled around in proximity to it.

From such fine distinctions are legends made... but Peary was adamant that he was the first person there, and if you look it up, his name tends to always pop up first.

There is some supposition that Peary was deliberately obstructive when it came to furnishing evidence of his claim. Genuinely being sure he had arrived at the pole is one thing...

knowing he probably didn't, and then lying about it - even by omission - is quite another.

This isn't his primary claim to being an awful human being however. This comes in the form of his treatment of the Inuit people who helped his teams to polar success.

The Inuit folk had scant access to metal. What they did have came from an iron rock, *the Innaanganeq meteorite* - which was one of the largest of its type known to science. They would carve pieces of this off to make utensils and tools. This fascinated Peary... so he simply took it off them and took it back to America.

He dug up their ancestors - in front of them - and shipped them back to America for display in museums.

> *To the women's crying and the men's questioning he answered that he was taking our dead friends to a warm and pleasant land to bury them. Our sole supply of flint for lighting and iron for hunting and cooking implements was furnished by a huge meteorite. This Peary put aboard his steamer and took from my poor people, who needed it so much.*
> *- Minuk (P. Petrone 1992, Northern Voices)*

He also took back a number of inuit people, several of whom died of tuberculosis after being kept in appalling conditions. One father and son - Qisuk and his child Minik - were tricked into going to America on the pretense of gathering tools and weapons (for hunting) for the tribe.

When Qisuk died, Minik was shown a fake funeral, and Qisuk's body was instead autopsied and put up for display in the American Museum for Natural History. Minik found this out years later, in what I can imagine was one of the most horrifying museum visits in history.

Polar historian Fergus Fleming said of Peary that he was:

> *"Undoubtedly the most driven, possibly the most successful and probably the most unpleasant man in the annals of polar exploration."*

His claims to have reached the Geographic North Pole are controversial at best... but his treatment of the Inuit who helped him is fairly clear cut.

VINCENZO PERUGGIA (1881-1925)

The Mona Lisa is a portrait painting by Italian artist Leonardo da Vinci. It was painted some time between 1503 and 1517, and is considered "the best known, the most visited, the most written about, the most sung about, the most parodied work of art in the world".

Anyone who has gone to see it in The Louvre, Paris, will know that it is disappointingly small, and surprisingly brown. Nevertheless, it is one of the most famous paintings in the world. It is valued somewhere in the region of half a billion US dollars.

It has hung in the Louvre since 1797. Well... almost. It was actually stolen in 1911.

Our lad Vincenzo Peruggia perpetrated what could be considered the greatest art theft in history... if it wasn't for the fact that it was hardly a stellar plan and was based on some rather silly misunderstandings.

Peruggia claims that he thought the painting was stolen from his home country, Italy, by Napoleon, during the French emperor's reign a century earlier.

Napoleon had certainly plundered his way through Italy's galleries and was not at all shy about returning to France with his Misbegotten Booty[89], but the Mona Lisa was not one of them. The Italian painting had actually been gifted to King Francis I by none other than the Leonardo himself, when the painter moved to France at the tail end of the 16th century.

Peruggia had heard tell of Napoleon's jackdaw-like acquisitive nature while working legitimately as a handyman at The Louvre, put two and two together, and had come up with The Mona Lisa... and Wikipedia not being a thing back then, he had no online sources to fact-check.

As a patriotic Italian, he decided to take the painting back shortly before his 30th birthday.

The incredibly detailed plan went as follows: (You may wish to take notes, it gets pretty convoluted from here.)

He waited until the gallery was empty, walked up to the painting, and stuck it up his smock. Then he walked out.

Um... yeah. One of the most expensive and famous paintings of all time, and he basically just took it off the wall, bunged it up his anorak, and whistled nonchalantly as he sauntered out the front door, waving goodbye to Mabel at the front desk.

I for one would have been sweating bullets had I got something so famous (and likely to get me into trouble) jammed up my cardie. Whatever we have to say about the (lack of) intricacy of Peruggia's scheme, he must have had nerves of steel.

Then he simply dropped off the radar for two years.

During these years, I like to think that Peruggia had $600 million worth of fine art just leaning against the wall above his mantlepiece, while he made his tea and listened to Marconi's Greatest Hits on his wireless.

He probably kept it in a box.

So, we move on two years, to the period in which we can assume that Peruggia, in all his patriotic fervour, would have handed the recovered painting back to the Italian art fraternity, yes? Having returned it from the clutches of the Napoleonic foe?

Not a bar of it, no.

He tried to sell it to Alfredo Geri, a gallery owner in Florence. Geri, not being an idiot, knew that there was absolutely no way in hell he wanted to be found in possession of one of the hottest pieces of stolen art. He immediately contacted the Polizia, who couldn't believe their luck, and Peruggia was arrested.

The fact that Peruggia tried to sell the painting does suggest that his motivations weren't as pure as he made out... or it's possible that he realised (post-theft) that he'd made a rather large error, and just wanted to cash in... but either way... he was caught.

The Italian government eventually (after an Italian tour) returned the painting to France, and there it has remained - vandalised several times, but never again stolen - as it hangs in The Louvre once more.

As for Peruggia... even with the question of motivation hanging over him, the court decided he was a misguided patriot rather than a hardened criminal and sentenced him to one year and fifteen days imprisonment. He served no more than seven months... being hailed by the general populace in Italy as a bit of a lovable rogue.

There's a lot to be said for being a lovable rogue. Just imagine what you could get away with if people tended to just shake their head amusedly at you and go "Oh, what is he like!" rather than demand you be banged up in the slammer for the rest of your life.

He later served in World War I, was captured, and spent two further years as a prisoner in Austro-Hungary. He died in 1925 on his 44th birthday. Possibly a misguided patriot... possibly a short-sighted opportunist who just happened to pick the wrong fence... but a villain and a rogue in the finest tradition.

PIERRE POIVRE (1719-1786)

It's the 1700s, and the Dutch control the flow of spice to the West... and the spice must flow. Their grip on the spice trade was absolute, and anyone caught smuggling live plants or seeds was summarily executed.

The big one was nutmeg, but there were other spices. In the 15th century, the Dutch had control over several of the only islands in Indonesia where these spices grew. Their control was brutal, and one governor went so far as to behead and dismember several dozen truculent indigenous chieftains after negotiations over a fort construction broke down.

The locals were treated as slave labour at best, and life under Dutch rule would likely not have been particularly pleasant for them.

Needless to say, spices were big money. Empire building money. The Dutch, the French, and the English were at loggerheads over the whole thing, and the Dutch-controlled islands were the powerbase around which the bulk of the spice trade rotated.

The Dutch maintained their monopoly for two and a half centuries, in the face of fierce opposition.

Enter Pierre Poivre.

He was a fairly diminutive Frenchman, and a missionary by trade. He had in his life travelled to all places East, including India, China, and Indochina, and through this developed an interest in trade.

His mercantile interests were aroused, and after a rather unfortunate incident in Vietnam in which he kidnapped a young Vietnamese person to serve as his interpreter, he and all other European 'missionaries' were kicked out of the country.

He was at one point arrested in China and had to teach himself Chinese in order to defend himself.

He was made prisoner several times in several places but managed to wrangle his way out of trouble with some alacrity. Had a bit of a gift for it, by all accounts.

Some time post-China, he was travelling back to France, when his ship came under attack by British forces, and he lost an arm when a cannonball snicked it right off.

An almost fatal blow in an era that knew nothing of antibiotics, Poivre retired to nearby Indonesia to recuperate. With little else to do, he kept a weather eye on the local trade.

> Poivre had been a tireless collector of intelligence on the islands, and his sources informed him of the discovery of a small, uninhabited island northwest of Ternate called Miao, where spices grew in abundance and the Dutch were not especially vigilant as to its security.
> - Charles Corn (1998). A Narrative of the Spice Trade

Some years later, Poivre arranged clandestine forays into the Dutch spice islands - Miao especially - and acquired several thousand clove and nutmeg seeds and seedlings. These he smuggled across hostile seas to French-friendly islands, such as (but not exclusively) Reunion, Mauritius, and the Seychelles, and not too long afterwards the Dutch spice monopoly was a thing of the past.

To the French, he was a heroic figure. To the Dutch, I am sure he was a brigand, a villain, and a vagabond, with a name wreathed in angst and ire.

Nobody comes out of the spice wars smelling of roses, unfortunately. The sheer amounts of money involved turned colonisation into a massive commercial enterprise, and corporations care very little about people.

The loss of the monopoly was a massive blow to the Dutch East India company, and the Dutch as a global power, so much was invested in the spice trade. It certainly wasn't the end of their power, but it definitely signalled a decline in fortune, and a massive economic boost for France.

The Poivre Islands coral atoll is named in his honour. They can be found in the coral islands and atolls that belong to the Seychelles.

The Anglicised version of Piere is "Peter", and the surname Poivre means "Pepper" in French. This has led some historians to suggest that he was the subject of the rather long-lived "Peter Piper" tongue twister:

> *Peter Piper picked a peck of pickled peppers.*
> *A peck of pickled peppers Peter Piper picked.*
> *- S. Hassall; P.J.Hassall (1988). Exploration, Discovery and Settlement*

CHARLES PONZI (1882-1949)

It's likely that most people will recognise the name Charles Ponzi. He was one of the early big swindlers of the 20th century, and the scheme for which he is known - the Ponzi Scheme - financially ruined a lot of people.

PONZI'S EARLY LIFE

Ponzi was born in 1882 in Italy, to a family that had titles, but which had since fallen on hard times. Charles himself took a job as a postal worker, before being accepted to university in Rome.

University didn't go well for Ponzi. Because his family had inherited titles, Ponzi had many wealthy friends at university. Alas, his income was nevertheless practically nil. Given that his friends saw university as a vacation, Ponzi ended his time at university with no money, and more critically, no degree.[90]

The previous few decades had seen a lot of emigration to the United States, and formerly poor Italians were now returning as rich men, with New World money. Ponzi decided that he would try the same, and set sail for the Americas, arriving in 1903 with $2.50 in his pocket.

LIFE OUTSIDE ITALY

He did odd jobs for a while before landing his first real job - as a waiter - but was quickly fired for theft.[91]

Deciding that America wasn't working out for him, Ponzi shifted to Canada, and managed to blag himself into a job in a bank. Not just any bank, but a bank that was set up purely to serve the needs of the massive influx of Italian immigrants arriving in Canada.

It was the dubious goings-on at the bank which gave Ponzi the idea for his nefarious big schemes... and sure enough, the bank failed, with the bank's CEO stealing the bulk of the money and fleeing to Mexico.

I've often wondered how this worked in an era where money wasn't handled digitally. I mean, we're clearly talking about millions of dollars here, and it would almost certainly have had to have been shipped as actual hardware in crates or something. This seems a lot more risky than simply bouncing the transaction through a bunch of shell corporations until it lands in some account somewhere in the Caymans.

Ponzi bounced around Montreal for a while doing odd jobs, until he found a chequebook unattended at a business, and wrote himself a check for over $400. He was caught for this and spent three years in prison. He told his mother that he was working at the prison, rather than imprisoned in it, as the 'special assistant' to the warden.

Upon his release, Ponzi decided that Canada was, if anything, worse for him than America, so he decided to move back south of the border and start again. Unfortunately, he was unable to resist attempting to make a few extra dollars smuggling illegal immigrants from Canada into America, and as a result spent two years in prison in Atlanta.

It was here that Ponzi met a chap by the name of Charles Morse, a Wall Street businessman and market speculator. Morse became something of a role-model to Ponzi and taught him things about the business of Finance that really turned his life around... sort of. Upon his release, he moved to Boston.

THE SCHEME STARTS

After beetling around for a bit in various jobs, and trying to pull various schemes, Ponzi started his own company, called the "Securities Exchange

Company", and began to promote a money-making scheme offering significant return on investment.

In today's world, he might have preferred to bandy about words like "blockchain" and "monkeys" or something... but I guess things worked differently back then, when nobody knew what an NFT was (OK, so kind-of like now) and "crypto" was just somewhere you buried the "bodyo".

He claimed that he could double investment within 90 days... and certainly, early adopters made a great deal of money from Ponzi's plans.

Ponzi hired agents and paid them generously with commissions for every dollar they raised from investors. By the end of July 1920, the scheme had gone viral, and Ponzi's company was raking in around a million dollars a day (Approximately US$14.46 million in today's money).

People were being paid. Profits were enormous. Word spread, and soon people were investing their life savings and mortgaging their houses to buy into Ponzi's financial nirvana.

The problem was that Ponzi was not making new money. The only way he could pay off his earlier investors was to find increasing numbers of new investors. While the number of investors was skyrocketing, Ponzi's scheme was working like a charm.

Many people chose not to withdraw their profits, but re-invested them in the scheme, hoping to accumulate even more profit... something which worked quite comfortably with Ponzi's plans.

Ponzi, of course, was living very well indeed. He bought property, had rather large accounts in several banks, purchased a few companies, and... it must be said... did try to use those companies to generate profits to repay his investors.

However, he had a financial tiger by its tail. There was absolutely no way he was going to be able to provide the promised profits to all of those investors, and the more people who invested, the worse things got, because while there was more money coming in, there was also a lot more which needed to be paid out.

THINGS START TO GO BAD

However, Ponzi's rags-to-riches story was starting to attract attention, and people were beginning to doubt that his business practices were sound, and were - in fact - potentially immoral, even if legal.

Eventually, the US Attorney for the District of Massachusetts - Daniel Gallagher - commissioned an audit of Ponzi's company books. Then incriminating documents were found that suggested Ponzi was not generating profits at all but was simply 'robbing Peter to pay Paul', and it all started to fall apart.

People began demanding their money. Ponzi was paying out money at an alarming rate... money which he barely had left in the grand scheme of things... and there was concern that a run on Ponzi's reserves could turn into a major headache for banking in general.

Then the news broke about Ponzi's criminal background, his time spent in prison, and the fact that he was millions in debt, and drawing on money he didn't have, because of his dealings with various financial institutions.

Then the audit results were made public, and Ponzi was charged with mail fraud. He surrendered to the Police - his empire fallen, and with it six banks in total, and all of his investors were receiving little more than a third of their initial investments back. A total of $20 million was lost - which is around $200 million in today's money.

IN AND OUT OF PRISON

Here's the surprising thing... he was sentenced to only five years in federal prison and was released after only three and a half. He was immediately charged again with larceny - much to his surprise - and was sentenced to an additional seven years as a "common and notorious thief".

Upon his release, he moved to Florida, and seeking to capitalise on the Florida land boom, began selling tracts of land to investors, promising massive returns on investment. This was, of course, another scam, and he was basically selling useless swampland to gullible people. He was again charged and convicted with violating trust and securities laws... but during the process of appeal, when he was released on a bond... he tried to escape the United States on a merchant ship heading for Italy.

He was, unfortunately for him, caught in New Orleans before the ship left US waters, and he was again imprisoned. This time until 1934. Ponzi was deported back to Italy as an undesirable later that year.

THE END OF PONZI

Ponzi lived as a translator in Italy for the remainder of his life. He had a heart-attack in 1941, and a stroke a few years later which left him almost completely blind and paralysed down his left side. He died in 1949.

Was he apologetic at all? On his deathbed, Ponzi told an American reporter:

> *"Without malice aforethought, I had given them the best show that was ever staged in their territory since the*

landing of the Pilgrims!"

CAROLINE PRODGERS (MID 1800S)

The strange tale of a rather unpleasant old lady involves the heiress to a considerable fortune, and a terror to cab drivers in 19th century London.

There are plenty of crotchety old individuals throughout history, but few have gained a such niche, but enduring, reputation as Caroline Prodgers, who became a bane upon public transport in London.

THE SCENE IS SET

In the 19th century there were nearly seven million people living in London. It was one of the largest cities in the British Empire, and one of the most popular ways of getting about (apart from walking) was the Hansom Cab.

This, like a modern-day taxi, was a vehicle that you could flag down, and take from one place to another. A two-wheeled 'cab' drawn by a single horse, and the 'cabbie' who was expected to have a near encyclopaedic knowledge of London's streets.

CAROLINE'S LITIGIOUS HISTORY

Caroline's first recorded brushes with the law came during a messy divorce process. She attempted to not only divorce, but completely disinherit her Austrian sea-captain husband. She even went so far as to claim that her children were not his... something which was so incredibly scandalous in the day, that it became big news.

Her husband was ultimately entitled to a divorce settlement, which Caroline refused to pay. She was also taken to court because she refused to pay the shorthand-writer she had employed during the divorce. She had clearly become quite *au-fait* with the legal process, because this was the start of her long and fabled career as a litigant.

So obsessed was she with taking people to court that she sued her own cook for singing on the job. She instigated a physical fight with a newspaper publisher after refusing to pay for the publication, and then sued him when her dress got torn in the scuffle. A watchmaker delivered an incorrect watch to her house, and next thing he knew, he had a court date.

Any slight, no matter how small, was met with

a letter from a solicitor, and a date at court... usually with no prior communication to attempt to settle matters in a less vindictive manner.

THE CAB DRIVERS

Nobody really knows why cab drivers were so frequently in Caroline's headlights. She clearly seemed to have some kind of special hatred for the breed and seemed almost gleeful in her attempts to drag them into court for the tiniest of perceived infractions.

She certainly didn't seem to mind using their services - as frequently as she could - but did not like to pay them full fare. She would stop them scant meters short of being able to charge her full fare... she would cross-check to make sure they had taken what she saw as the most efficient route... she would time them... she would default on payment as much as she could, and if there was the slightest hint of insurrection on their behalf...

... well, she would happily have them arrested, and took more than fifty of them to court. She won most of the cases, largely because the prevailing wind blew in favour of the customer, and because the cabbies would - on occasion - certainly take a liberty or two.

It is said that it took a lot to phase a London cabbie. In a world where life was cheap and crime was rife, cabbies were more frightened of Caroline Prodger than they were of cutthroats and ne'er-do-wells.

They would genuinely whisper tales in hushed tones about her, bemoan the fate of her latest victims, and if any of them saw her coming, they'd shout "Mother Prodgers!", and immediately every driver in the area would flee the scene. So hated was she that during the Guy Fawkes festival, the cabbies would gather and burn an effigy of the woman.

So fed up were the judges of the day that one stood up in court and suggested that if she had such issue with the cab drivers in London - and given she was a remarkably wealthy woman in her own right - perhaps she could see her way clear to purchasing her own carriage.

This naturally fell on deaf ears, and the reign of terror continued for over twenty years... becoming the stuff of legend.

DEATH AND LEGACY

It is said that the first attempts to make a reliable fare-meter were because of Caroline, and the cabbie's attempts to find a solution to her constant ongoing penny-pinching and litigant-diplomacy.

When she died in 1890, few cabbies were sorry to see her go... though several were said to have offered free trips to her funeral.

Her obituary read:

> *Mrs. Caroline Giacometti Prodgers, the terror of London cabmen, is dead. Her habit was to drive the fullest possible distance for the money, pay the exact legal fare, and then cause the arrest of the cabman for expressing his feelings.*

She could be hailed as a somewhat eccentric campaigner for the consumer, because there's no doubt that many cab drivers back in the day would take a foot if you gave them an inch... but she is, perhaps unfortunately, widely hailed as the villainous shadow haunting the nightmares of the hard-working individuals who kept the arteries of London flowing.

So obsessed was she with taking people to court that she sued her own cook for singing on the job. She instigated a physical fight with a newspaper publisher after refusing to pay for the publication, and then sued him when her dress got torn in the scuffle.

JAMES QUIN (1693-1766)

A boisterous, angry man, and no stranger to a scuffle, James Quin was an English actor of some repute, but more than that, he was a menace to himself and others.

The grandson of the Lord Mayor of Dublin, and the illegitimate son of an Irish-born Barrister[92], born in London, Quin was almost - but not quite - wealthy. Being illegitimate, he was unable to claim a family inheritance.

In 1710, at age 17, he began his acting career. In 1715 he was being mentioned in local publications as an actor of no small skill. His Falstaff (a Shakespearean character) was considered absolutely sublime.

As his fame grew, so did his obstreperousness, and his viciously sarcastic tongue-lashings were almost considered a rite of passage among young actors. He was notoriously quick to anger and shouted more than he spoke.

He was also, as it happened, an accomplished swordsman who practiced regularly.

At one point an actor mispronounced a character's name on-stage, and Quin - ever the grouch - berated him at length about it. It almost came to blows, and the other actor - William Bowen - made the mistake of challenging Quin to a duel. Quin slew him with his sword and was subsequently convicted of manslaughter.

Oddly, this was not considered to be a significant problem back in the early 1700s, and Quin was barely punished as a result.

Now, this likely made for quite the awkward employment situation. It certainly doesn't foster a safe working environment when one of your fellow actors - provoked or not - could cut you down where you stood... and then be seen to get away with it with little more than a slap on the wrist.[93]

The awkwardness would no doubt have got much worse when another young actor - perhaps a bit simple in the head department, or at least significantly less able to read the room full of people making desperate "NONONONONO!" gestures - decided to become angered by Quin's relentless sarcasm and criticism and physically attacked him.

Quin drew his sword and killed him too.

This resulted in more or less the same legal outcome. While Quin had technically provoked both incidents by being a complete turd-helmet to someone, he had also technically not thrown the first punch in either case - so according to the law of the day his totally disproportionate violent response was... acceptable.

In 1721 a drunken noble stormed onto the stage to assault the theatre manager, and Quin drew his sword, and... well, you see how this goes. Quin was a bit of a loose unit and rather free with his sword. This latest little escapade resulted in a riot, and Quin was forced to defend the stage with his sword until the local authorities turned up to restore order. Tensions were so high after this that King George I decreed that all theatres would have an armed guard until further notice... a situation that persisted for some time.

His fame as an actor, however, continued to grow, and it was in the 1750s that he became the highest ever paid actor at the time, with an annual salary of £1,000. That's about £232,862 in today's money. (US$307,381)

He wasn't completely awful, however. He was noted to be quite generous to those he admired, and if you could stomach his constant criticism, he was otherwise quite supporting of young actors trying to get a foothold in the art.

Eventually he retired to Bath[94], where he lived quite happily keeping late hours, with much eating and drinking until his death in early 1766. Sometimes being a total cluster of rodent gonads pays dividends, it seems.

RABODOANDRIANAMPOINIMERINA (1778-1861)

In 1828 the sovereign ruler of Madagascar was a Queen who assumed control after her young husband, Radama I, died. While she was born Rabodoandrianampoinimerina, fortunately, she was also known as Ranavalona, which will make my life an awful lot easier as I type this up. She was a brutal and bloody tyrant.

The Kingdom of Madagascar - which was formally known by the people who lived there as the Kingdom of Imerina - under her rule developed a large standing army, which Ranavalona wielded with significant force and authority.

The kingdom did not cover the whole of Madagascar, so the sovereign was quite enthusiastic about making sure that it did... so her standing army would travel to her borders to... convince... people that coming under her rule might be the wiser option.

Ranavalona was not a huge fan of the European super-powers of the time - particularly France - who she felt had taken rather a lot of advantage of her people over the years. - and absolutely did not approve of English missionaries who were attempting to convert her people to Christianity.

THE FRENCH

French interests were expansionistic. Already under control of several small islands near Madagascar, they wanted control of the main island body to (a) ease their route to India, and (b) deprive England of the same.

After Ranavalona started severing ties with European powers, her ability to obtain modern weaponry was significantly diminished, and the French decided to attempt a landing. They were driven off by Ranavalona's forces but retained enough people on the island to draw the sovereign into negotiations, which they hoped to swing to their advantage.

Ranavalona - quite cleverly - kept stalling until the French were absolutely riddled with malaria, which was endemic on the island, and then suggested they depart - with some alacrity - before she sent her troops in to mop up the mess.

This seemed to work, and the French took a large

step back, and from this point onwards their interaction with the Kingdom tended to be a lot more diplomatic than military.

THE ENGLISH

The English had a more subtle approach to expanding their influence in the kingdom.

English missionaries had entered the Kingdom while Radama I was alive, and with his blessing had started schools and initiated the teaching of industry. Of course, as is the way of things, they were heavily pushing Western culture as the only way to live.

Ranavalona was initially quite happy to let the missionaries carry on, and under her rule they introduced the Malagasy translations of the New Testament and expanded schooling and book production.

It was all going well until Ranavalona came under pressure from her own missionary-educated politicians to adopt a more Anglo-centric approach to life. She realised that people wanted to forsake the old ways, abandon their ancestors, forget their traditions, and become a sort-of second-class Little England... and she wasn't going to have a bar of it.

Acknowledging all the good that had been done to educate her people, Ranavalona told the missionaries that they were welcome to stay, but that all religious education must stop. Many actually did leave, rather than give up their proselytising. A few did not, and those who did maintained contact with leaders within the community to continue to push their agenda.

It's at this point that Ranavalona stepped from hard-nosed no-nonsense stern-faced ruler of a small Kingdom to murderous tyrant with a streak of the Machiavellian about her.

THE MADAGASCAN WAR ON CHRISTIANITY

Ranavalona decreed that anyone found in possession of a Bible, or who worshiped in congregation, or who continued to profess adherence to Christianity were - depending on context and circumstance - fined, jailed, manacled, subjected to trial by ordeal, or executed.

The last two were the default. If you were a rich noble, then you might get away with a little jail time and forfeit of all of your lands and money. Johnny Public, however, with barely two beans to rub together, was going to have a much harder time of it.

Community members still in contact with the missionaries reported the public execution of more than a dozen Christian leaders. Upon their refusal to renounce their new religion, they were dangled on ropes 50m above a jagged ravine for a while before the ropes were cut... sending them plummeting to their deaths.

Many more were stripped of land and title, forced into hard labour, or forced to undergo the Tangena Ordeal, which I will come to shortly. How true these reports were is subject to some debate, but it's clear that Ranavalona was comfortable with brutality to make a point which had otherwise been ignored.

THE TANGENA ORDEAL

Tangena is the name of a tree in Madagascar which produced seeds containing incredibly toxic *cardiac glycoside cerberin*.

If you want to maintain order as a tyrant, fear is a powerful tool in which to invest time and energy. If you were accused of wrongdoing, you would likely not have to undergo a protracted and costly trial... you'd simply be fed the toxin, and three pieces of chicken skin.

If you vomited up all three pieces of chicken skin, you were innocent, and could go about your business. If you didn't... or if you died because you'd just consumed a horrible toxin... then you were clearly guilty. If you hadn't died, at this point you'd be put to death anyway.

Ranavalona was a great believer in this method of proving guilt or innocence, and anyone could accuse anyone else. If you were accused of certain things - regardless of evidence - trial by Tangena was mandatory.

If you had been in a dispute with your neighbour, for example... let's say about mowing your lawn at 5am on a Sunday... he could turn around and accuse you of being a Christian... and your goose, as they say, was likely cooked.

Literally thousands of people died of Tangena poisoning during Ranavalona's reign. In 1838 alone, only ten years into her 33-year rule, an estimated 100,000 people were killed by the ordeal. That's one out of every five people in the kingdom at the time.

THE GREAT BUFFALO HUNT

As the story goes, in 1845 Ranavalona demanded that her entire royal court accompany her to hunt buffalo in the wilds of the Kingdom. A huge number of servants and slaves were brought along because - let's face it - nobles don't want to do all the heavy lifting.

Around fifty-thousand people started the hunt, travelling light and ordered to build a road as they went. The conditions were so bad that as many as ten thousand were thought to have died from disease, hunger, and exhaustion during the four-month ordeal.

It's possible that this hunt had an ulterior motive. Certainly, it wasn't the hunting of buffalo, because reportedly none were ultimately killed... but the road proved to be extremely beneficial, and nothing makes a point about your ability to wield supreme power than your willingness to use it to prove a point.

Many felt that this was evidence that Ranavalona was going mad, but who's going to make that point in an environment when the merest suggestion that you were not loyal could result in you being ritually poisoned.

LEGACY

In 1861, after 33 years of tyrannical rule full of intrigue and violent oppression, Ranavalona died in her sleep, and her son assumed the throne as King Radama II.

He almost immediately reversed all her policies, which had been roundly reviled by the international community... not to mention the people of the kingdom... who now celebrated like there was no tomorrow because, for the first time in 33 years it seemed like there actually might be.

Ranavalona was absolutely a remarkably able politician who successfully shielded her nation from European encroachment in an era when Europe was running rough-shod over the world... but she was also a remarkably cruel and xenophobic tyrant - and was possibly quite mad.

GRIGORI YEFIMOVICH RASPUTIN (1869-1916)

Grigor Rasputin was something of a religious zealot, seen by some as a prophet, and by others as a charlatan. He rose to prominence in Russia and strode among the last of the tsars.

Born a peasant generally meant that you'd die a peasant, but at this time the class system in Russia was all over the place, and Rasputin had a way with words. He became a wandering pilgrim after a religious epiphany in 1897, and after captivating an audience of religious and social leaders, was able to obtain an audience with both Emperor Nicholas and Empress Alexandra towards the end of 1905.

The Imperial duo's son was afflicted with haemophilia, and Rasputin was able to wrangle his way into a position of healer for the child.[95]

This was a position of some influence, and while Rasputin was highly regarded in the eyes of the imperials, he was dogged by scandal. He traded influence for bribes and sexual favours and worked very hard to increase his courtly standing.

There were rumours of all sorts of wrongdoing, from sexual assault to religious heresy, and even unsubstantiated rumours that he had been having an affair with the tsarina.

He was certainly a dishevelled looking fellow, who really was not a fan of personal hygiene. He would preach to his audience about how womanising was the key to spiritual salvation.

Unfortunately for him his influence in the court was seen as a threat to the nobility - many of whom suspected the tsar and tsarina were mere puppets who had been hypnotised by this odious individual.

The onset of World War I saw Rasputin's star rise in the court, while his popularity waned further among the nobility, as Russia suffered defeat after defeat. Waned, in fact, to the point that someone *basically* said:

> *"You know what? I've had enough of this faux-monastic dickhead. It's time someone took him to the goddamn*

cleaners, and that someone, is going to be..."

Chionya Guseva

A Russian peasant herself, Guseva was a follower of a rival of Rasputin... a priest who had formerly followed him before deciding that Rasputin was having an awful lot of rampant sex for a religious man and disavowed him.

Guseva stabbed Rasputin in the stomach. She said she did it on her own, but the scuttlebutt around the land was that she had been put up to it either by the rival, or by some other figure about the court. She was found 'not guilty' by reason of insanity, for... well, quite frankly, poor Chionya Guseva was a bit... suggestible.

It was thought that Rasputin was going to die, but he pulled through... a testament, some said, to his piety.

So, some nobles had a bit of a think, and decided that the influence Rasputin wielded in the court was an appalling ongoing situation, him being from peasant stock and all. They decided:

"Stabbing is apparently too good for him. Let's make absolutely sure that he doesn't survive the next attempt. We'll start with cyanide, move to other poisons, and finish him off with a bullet. We should enlist the services

of..."

Prince Felix Yusupov and Grand Duke Dmitri Pavlovich

So, Rasputin was invited to dinner at Yusupov's place.

He was given cake laced with cyanide, which he ate, and apparently suffered no ill effects from. He was given wine laced with various other poisons, and merely became a trifle gassy. At this point, it was looking pretty good that maybe there was something to this monkly-piety malarky after all.

Yusupov, somewhat surprised that Rasputin was still working his way through the madeira, popped upstairs where Pavlovich was hiding and confessed that he didn't know what to do at this point. So Pavlovich grabbed a revolver (let's face it, Imperial Russia... firearms were probably not in short supply), went downstairs, and shot Rasputin through the chest.

This merely seemed to enrage Rasputin, and he leapt up and attacked the man, and chased him into a nearby courtyard, where Pavlovich shot him twice more, including once at point blank range through the forehead. There's not a lot of coming back from that, regardless of how pious you are... and that was the end of Rasputin.

They wrapped his body in a blanket, and dumped it into a river which was, somewhat unfortunately, frozen solid. His body therefore went 'thud' instead of 'splish'[96], and was subsequently found nearby not long afterwards.[97]

He was buried the next day surrounded by his imperial 'family', but his wife, mistress, and children were not allowed to attend. He was dug up not too long afterwards and burned to avoid his gravesite being used as a rally-point for rebels.

GÉRAUD RÉVEILHAC (1851-1937)

World War I was a disaster for anyone involved. The stale military bureaucracy had not adapted to the recent advances in weaponry, and massed charges towards waiting machineguns were not uncommon. Casualties were horrific and numerous.

Réveilhac was born in France, and graduated from the Special Military School of Saint-Cyr as a sub-lieutenant in the French army.

He was praised for his early actions in putting down an uprising in west-central France, and actions on mainland southeast Asia in the latter part of the 1800s. He was ultimately made a general in 1909, not too many years before World War I broke out. It is during this period that the Réveilhac gained most of his infamy.

In March 1915, Réveilhac ordered troops under his command - specifically the 21st company of the 336th Infantry Regiment - to make a bayonet charge against a German machinegun position.[98]

Unfortunately, immediately before the attack began, the artillery which was supposed to soften up the machinegun nests instead bombarded the French forces, killing many and injuring others.[99] The totally untouched German machineguns quickly obliterated the rest of the first wave as the depleted forces stormed into the mass of craters and barbed wire of No Man's Land.[100]

Unsurprisingly, the shellshocked second wave, which had already sustained artillery damage, and seen their comrades cut down by massed machinegun fire, refused to leave the trenches. When Réveilhac heard this, he was incensed, and ordered his artillery to shell his own men, to drive them out of the trenches and towards the enemy lines.[101]

Fortunately, the artillery commander (Colonel Raoul Berube) refused to obey without a written order, which - surprise, surprise - Réveilhac was unwilling to provide.

After the assault, Réveilhac had the entire second wave forces tried in a military court for failing to obey orders. Twenty-four men were sentenced to death for failing to obey the order to attack, and while 20 were given a stay of execution, four were executed as an example to the others - chosen by lottery.

Only a few days after the failed assault, four corporals were sent into No Man's Land to cut barbed wire when they came under heavy fire when the promised smoke bombardment never arrived. They barely made it back to the trenches alive, intending to head back out when the smoke shells landed... but the smoke never came.

Réveilhac ordered that the four men be executed. It was fairly clear that he had little to no regard for his troops, and that the realities of 'modern' warfare were not making their way through his impression of 'how things should be done'.

Another incident saw him ordering troops to relaunch a failed attack, while stating to a subordinate that he was still within acceptable limits for friendly casualties and could spare them if necessary.

In February 1916 he was eventually relieved of duty and forced to take leave. According to a letter sent in confidence by another general, it was felt that Réveilhac "seems to have arrived at the limit of his physical and intellectual capacity".

While he was not relieved of *all* command, he

never saw active service again, and was given a command in the reserves for the rest of the war. Upon completion of the war, General Réveilhac was made *Grand Officier of the Légion d'honneur*, and retired to his estates in western France.

Retiring in honour for someone who was so cavalier with the lives of his men does not seem fair... but things did come back to bite Réveilhac in the early 1920s when his actions were revealed with the public release of some military documents.

He was scandalised and condemned in both the public and the military press, and while he did write a letter to try to defend himself, it was censored by the Minister of War, who felt that it would only add fuel to the anti-Réveilhac fire at this point.

Hardly justice, given the nature of his disdain for his troops. Réveilhac eventually died of natural causes in 1937 in his home in Nantes.

ZHENG YI SAO (1775-1844)

Zheng Yi Sao (also known as Ching Shih) was a Chinese pirate leader who was active in the South China Sea in the early years of the 1800s.

At the height of her power, Ching Shih commanded over 400 sailing vessels and around 50,000 pirates, all part of the Guangdong Pirate Confederation. Her ships would prey upon the trading vessels of many major powers, such as the East India Company, the Portuguese Empire, and the Qing Dynasty, out of China.

TAKING POWER

She didn't start out as the leader of the confederation. Growing up poor in Guangdong province, she worked at one point as a prostitute in a floating brothel.

At the age of 26, Ching Shih met and married Zheng Yi, who was the former leader of the pirates. He and his adopted son Zhang Bao basically ruled the waves around quite a large part of the South China Sea in the tail-end of the 1700s and start of the 1800s. It was when Zheng Yi up and died that thing got a bit hairy. Had the leadership gone to someone else within the faction, Ching Shih would probably have been killed.

As it stands, however, she married her former husband's adopted son to consolidate her position, and then took the reins of power herself. Her rule was brutal.

Any pirate who took too much initiative without following orders, or who flouted orders, or did basically anything that wasn't on the "approved things to do" list was immediately beheaded. It was a brave pirate indeed who did anything other than precisely what he was told, when he was told to do it, and the fear and awe she commanded was instrumental in retaining her position.

That, and the fact that she was actually very good at being a pirate.

THE PEARL RIVER RAIDS

The pirate confederation really stepped up its game after Ching Shih rose to power... culminating in the destruction of a good half of the Chinese provincial fleet and allowing the pirates access to the Pearl River network, and the rich - much plunderable - lands therein.

Numerous villages, settlements, and towns fell

victim to the rampaging pirates. Ching Shih and her lieutenants oversaw the slaughter of many thousands of people. It also saw a surge in recruiting, and the acquisition of quite a few more ships. The pirate confederation was going from strength to strength, and things were looking decidedly grim for the provincial forces.

THE FINAL BATTLE

The last grand battle was the blockade of Tung Chung Bay, where a combined fleet of Chinese and Portuguese forces attacked the pirates as they anchored for repairs.

The battle waxed and waned, but ultimately turned into a blockade, as the combined forces of China and Portugal stopped the pirates from fleeing into open water or cruising back into the Pearl River where they would have the advantage of smaller vessels.

Worried that the blockade was turning into a stalemate, the leader of the combined forces launched fireships against the pirate fleet.

Of the forty-three fireships that were launched against the pirates, not even one found a target. Several were actually turned around as the wind shifted and set fire to two of the Sino-Portuguese fleet.

The pirates broke the blockade with the favourable wind, and easily slipped past their foes. The final tally of damage was around 46 ships (including the fireships), to none. The pirates were largely unscathed.

THE ODDS WERE SHIFTING

Trade with China was too lucrative to allow a bunch of rowdy pirates to control the oceans, so eventually the British, Chinese, and Portuguese forces all joined forces to tackle the pirate threat.

While Ching Shih was a capable commander, the combined naval might of several of the world's first super-powers was all but insurmountable, regardless of the loyalty she commanded. The pirate supply lines were ultimately cut off, and Ching Shih - aware of the changing tides - decided to get out while she still had some power to negotiate.

Timed well, but not without the occasional hiccup, negotiations for a cease-fire and ultimate surrender were underway... and 17,318 pirates, 226 ships, 1,315 cannons, and 2,798 assorted weapons were surrendered in April 1810. Ching Shih later sailed in with her personal retinue of 24 ships and 1,433 pirates and surrendered those as well.

POST SURRENDER, AND OUTCOMES

Ching Shih and her husband actually did quite well for themselves after giving up piracy.

Zhang Bao - the husband - joined forces with

the Provincial Chinese fleet and started mopping up those pirates and ships which had not surrendered. He advanced in rank in the fleet to colonel before succumbing to illness and dying in 1822.

In 1844, Zheng Yi Sao died, having become the proprietor of an infamous gambling house somewhere around Guangdong, where she had grown up.

Any pirate who took too much initiative without following orders, or who flouted orders, or did basically anything that wasn't on the "approved things to do" list was immediately beheaded.

IGNAZ SEMMELWEIS (1818-1865)

In 19th century, the heart of medical science beat most strongly in Vienna. It exerted international influence thanks to talent drawn from all corners of Europe. It sought to reinvent medical knowledge from the bottom up.

This philosophy attracted criticism, as it was said to favour science over patients, but it laid the foundations for modern surgery, and modern evidence-based medicine. While on the cusp of enlightenment, however, it was notoriously unwelcoming to some innovators – a hidebound response to poorly understood concepts.

IGNAZ SEMMELWEIS WAS SUCH AN INNOVATOR.

In 1847, Semmelweis discovered that there was a profound difference in mortality rates in two clinics at the Vienna general Hospital. There was a highly infectious disease called Puerperal Fever, which was killing many women who gave birth in the 19th century.

The first clinic had almost three times as many deaths from this disease than the second.

Semmelweis described desperate patients begging not to be put into the first clinic. Some patients even preferred to give birth outside the clinic, rather than be admitted, only attending the hospital for follow-up care, post procedure.

Semmelweis was surprised to note that almost none of these cases suffered from Puerperal Fever.

Both clinics were in the same hospital and had the same procedures. Semmelweis conducted meticulous research to eliminate all possible differences. The only real difference involved staffing of the clinics:

- **Clinic One**
  A teaching service for medical students
- **Clinic Two**
  Nurses Only

So, what was it about this difference that caused the disease?

The medical students would conduct post-mortem examinations of cadavers before doing their rounds. The nurses would not. Semmelweis hypothesized that the students were carrying "cadaverous particles" on their hands, and infecting patients. He instituted a policy of hand washing between autopsy work and the examination of patients.

THE MORTALITY RATE AT THE FIRST CLINIC DROPPED BY 90%

However, the germ theory of disease transmission was not yet accepted in Vienna. His hypothesis, and the results, were largely ignored, rejected, and ridiculed. He was dismissed from the hospital for political reasons and harassed by the medical community in Vienna.

He was ultimately committed to an asylum, and he died there of septicaemia only 14 days later, after being severely beaten by the asylum guards.

Semmelweis's practice only became widely accepted years after his death, when Louis Pasteur developed the germ theory of disease. Semmelweis is now considered a pioneer of antiseptic procedures, and doubtless has saved countless lives.

Semmelweis knew there was a serious problem, and he conducted research to find out what it was. He formulated a hypothesis, and a response to what he believed to be the cause of the problem. The results showed a significant improvement.

He did not need to know the mechanics of germ theory to form a model of disease transmission, and indeed his response proved to be sound. What he did not do well was manage the objections of his peers and superiors. He railed against the way they stuck to what they 'knew', and how they seemed to ignore his findings, leading to his downfall.

FU SHENG (355-357)

The dynastic state of Former Qin was once ruled by a young tyrant, who brought mayhem into a world which prided itself on order and control. Fu Sheng was never going to have a good ending.

Born Pu Sheng, third son of Pu Jiàn the founding father of the Former Qin dynasty, started out life as any emperor's son might. However, at an early age, he lost the sight on one eye. Some claimed it was due to being attacked by an eagle while he was collecting eagle eggs.

As he grew, he became increasingly fragile about his eye, and anyone who commented upon it would bear the brunt of his anger. At one point, he became so enraged at someone who said he could only cry from one eye, he burst the blind eye's intact eyeball and as the ichor dripped down his cheek he screamed "look upon the tears of my blind eye!"[102]

This does not bode well for his eventual imperial rule, as you can imagine. I certainly wouldn't vote for someone who pulled a stunt like that... but then folk have voted for worse, I suppose. One good point about tyrannical rule, I guess, is that at least the polling booths are never crowded.

He grew to be a ferocious warrior, and in the battles that protected the territories of Former Qin, he was personally very successful - defeating many of the opponent's top officers... but his command of men was poor, and he never excelled as a general.

His father then had the family name changed from Pu to Fu... which I suppose I can fully understand. I wouldn't want to go through life being called Pu either.

The now Fu Sheng was not first in line for the throne, but after his father had a dream about half-blind goats (Don't ask me. Anyone who bases their decision-making on dreams is more than a little dubious in my humble opinion.) he had Fu Sheng crowned emperor upon his death.

The first thing Fu Sheng did was decide to settle a few old scores.[103]

Before his death, Fu Jiàn had installed several assistants for his son, and Fu Sheng had most of them immediately executed. He then decided that certain words were henceforth to be illegal, and outlawed words like *missing, slanted, without, less*, and *lacking*... largely because he was a bit tetchy about people referring to his eye.

Some of those you could comfortably do without. I could probably go quite a long time without saying 'slanted' for example... but I've already used 'without', and the word 'less' is important in any economy. However, if you were caught using those words, you were immediately put to death.

It would have made more sense, perhaps, to say "if anyone mentions my eye, I'll knock their block off", and leave the lexicon alone, but you know tyrants!

Fu Sheng also spent a lot of time drinking - usually before holding court where officials would bring him important decisions that needed to be made. He would take great delight in giving them nonsensical or ridiculous decisions.

Need to decide between two noble families, each with a claim on a tract of land? Easy... have the heads of the two families clothed in rags and whipped out of town, before giving the land to a random passing peasant. It did not endear him to anyone... except maybe a random passing peasant.[104]

His uncle approached him at one point and suggested that it was unseemly for the ruler of a dynasty to behave in this manner. Rather than see the error of his ways, Fu Sheng had the top of the man's skull removed, like a boiled egg, and shortly thereafter executed him.

He also thought it amusing to throw live animals to cauldrons of boiling water, and had people skinned alive for minor infractions.

It should be fairly clear at this point - if it was not clear earlier - that we're not dealing with a normal person here who had simply let power go to his head. There was something clearly wrong with Fu Sheng, and the people around him were starting to decide that enough was enough.

Things started to come to a head when the northern border of Former Qin was attacked by General Yao Xiang - who wished to secure some buffer-space between Former Qin and his own independent state.

Fu Sheng's own generals fought off the attack, and killed Yao Xiang, securing the northern border, and protecting Former Qin from further aggression. The problem was that Fu Sheng not only did not reward his own generals, but he insulted them, and when one of them protested, he had them killed.

As well as all of this, Fu Sheng was quite paranoid. He believed that people were plotting against him. At first, this probably wasn't true, but in a sort-of self-fulfilling prophecy, he decided to preemptively kill off his cousins.

They were tipped off by Fu Sheng's ladies in waiting, and as a result, they waited until Fu Sheng was (again) drunk, and gathered their men together to attack the Imperial Palace.[105]

The Imperial Guard, whose job it is to protect the emperor, already resented how many of their men had been skinned alive, and immediately defected to the attacker's side... and Fu Sheng was effectively deposed.

The former emperor was sentenced to death, and sentence was carried out by dragging him behind a horse. One of the cousins subsequently became emperor, and led the Former Qin to its greatest glory, annexing several neighbouring provinces, and leading the empire to prosperity.

TOM SKELTON (1600S)

As our society gets more complex and our people get more complacent, the role of the jester is more vital than ever before. Please stop sitting around. We need you to make a ruckus.
- Seth Godin. American Author.

Having said that, we'll have none of that sort of shenanigans herein, thankyouverymuch. A jester is little more than a mime who is allowed to talk, and hit things with a bladder on a stick, and I shall have no truck with them... a reasonable position, as this tale of our latest remarkable person shall attest.

Tom Skelton - perhaps the original Tom Fool - was the jester at Muncaster castle in the 15th century (though exact times are a subject of some discussion).

Muncaster is now a privately owned castle in Cumbria, in England, overlooking the River Esk.

Back in the 1600s, it was the domain of Sir Alan Pennington, knight of the realm, and it was he who seems to have hired Skelton as jester.

As things go, you can imagine there was much jolly japery, and foolishness. Much ringing of bells and hitting of things with bladders on sticks. Probably one or two pies in faces... however these things work... but this particular jester - our Tom Skelton - was no simple jongleur.

It is said that he used to sit under a chestnut tree and offer directions to travellers. Those he took a dislike to, he sent toward a perilous and largely un-detectable lake of quicksand by the nearby cliffs, from which there was no chance of escape.

While possibly apocryphal, and certainly based on scant evidence, much of Tom's notoriety revolves around the night Sir Alan Pennington's unmarried daughter, Helwise, decided to go down to the nearby village in disguise, and dance with a local lad.

It seems this local lad - a carpenter's son, called Dick - was also her lover and a servant at the castle. Now, you can imagine the scandal. The daughter of a knight of the realm consorting with a common carpenter's son and servant? Heads would - quite literally - roll.

Word got out to another local knight, Sir Ferdinand, who wanted Helwise for himself. He, in turn, approached Tom Skelton... our villain in this tale. Skelton already had a bone to pick with Dick, as Dick had previously accused him of theft of money... so he decides to 'resolve' the issue rather permanently.

Tom Skelton, by all accounts, went down to the village and on the pretence of helping Dick elope with Helwise, got him drunk, bludgeoned him to death with his own tools, cut off his head, and proclaimed:

> *"I have hid Dick's head under a heap of shavings; and he will not find that so easily, when he awakes, as he did my shillings."*

And so easily murder was done.

The fallout of this act was unrecorded, but Sir Ferdinand did not get the lady in the end, Helwise preferring the nunnery. The knight himself fell in an unremarkable battle some time later.

After this act, there was no fool or jester at Muncaster for quite some time... but in recent years, a competition is held to find a new jester for the castle annually. You can but hope that they're not all villains.

There is actually a commissioned painting of Tom Skelton in his fool's attire, so we have an idea of what he looked like. In the full portrait, you can even see his own last-will and testament, in which he apparently predicts his own death while reportedly all but admitting to directing people to their doom.

JOHN SNOW (1813-1858)

London in the 1850s, there was an outbreak of cholera. This was a horrific disease which caused horrific diarrhoea, vomiting, cramps, and thirst. It killed a lot of people and made a great many more very sick in an age when most medicine was palliative.

Most in the medical profession were sold on the idea of *Miasma Theory*, which suggested that diseases were caused primarily by bad smells, and the Cthulhian effluvial horrors wafting up from the sewers on the wind. If you stayed away from bad smells, they figured, and sought clean air, you could avoid catching cholera.

Irritatingly, if you stay away from bad smells, you tend to stay away from many of the causes of disease, so at a fundamentally cursory level, this actually makes some sense. We know differently now, of course that while Miasma Theory wasn't *completely* wrong, the sewers and cesspits of London were the cause of the disease... not because of the smell, but because of the water.

People who had caught cholera - which originally came from the Indian subcontinent - the Ganges River specifically - would defecate in the usual manner[106], and the disease would enter the sewer system or a cesspit.

At this point, because of the age, overload, and poor construction of the original sewage system, the horrible filth would enter the water table, along with the bacteria that caused the disease.

The London epidemic had escalated quickly, and hundreds of people were dying. People were fleeing the city, and shops were closed.

London's water came primarily from a series of pumps which drew water up from underground. Many of these pumps were favoured over others, because the water tasted 'better'.

The physician John Snow was profoundly sceptical of the Miasma Theory, and took the next logical step of mapping all the houses where cholera was diagnosed. Through this, he realised that the Broad Street water pump - one favoured by many people - was right in the middle of the cluster.

Those who had caught the disease who lived a considerable distance from the pump seemed to cast doubt on the idea until the survivors were interviewed, and it seems they had water delivered to them specifically from the Broad Street pump because they preferred the taste.[107]

> *On proceeding to the spot, I found that nearly all the deaths had taken place within a short distance of the pump. There were only ten deaths in houses situated decidedly nearer to another street-pump. In five of these cases the families of the deceased persons informed me that they always sent to the pump in Broad Street, as they preferred the water to that of the pumps which were nearer.*
> *- Dr John Snow*

He showed his maps to the local council, who were initially convinced, and removed the handle from the pump.

The mortality rate started to bottom out, and the epidemic went into rapid decline. This became a foundation event in the science of epidemiology, and many lives were saved. Researchers discovered not much later that the public well had been dug only three feet from a cesspit, which had been leaking faecal bacteria into the water.

The problem was that - again - politics over-rode common sense in the face of public health. After the epidemic had subsided, officials replaced the handle on the pump, and rejected Snow's theory of germ transmission.

Nobody was happy with the thought of faecal-oral transmission of disease... and this was deemed far too unpleasant to trouble the public with.

Years later, little had changed in the area to resolve the problem, and while the outbreak never reached the heights it had in 1854, it was a clear and present danger for quite some time to come.

The value of Snow's diagnosis was not recognised until a dozen years later, when the investigation of *another* outbreak showed similar causes, and orders were issued that all drinking water was, from this point on, to be boiled. Boiling killed the bacteria outright.

Lots of people lived because the science was clear, and action was taken as a result. Lots of people died because those in power refused to see beyond the political expediencies once the going got a little tough.

Snow suffered a stroke while working in his London office on 10 June 1858. He was 45 years old at the time, and never got to see the accolades he received for his role as one of the founding fathers of epidemiology.

GEORGE SPENCER (1640S)

Science has done a lot for the human race, let's be fair. Sure, it has caused us some problems, too. Nobody really wants nuclear weapons, for example... but it is nice not to die of smallpox, and we now know how DNA works.

I do feel a bit sorry, however, for George Spencer, who was accused of fathering a one-eyed pig.

Yeah, the 1640s were replete with people who didn't know stuff that we consider fairly fundamental these days... but the depths of ignorance have yet to be plumbed... and frankly, people have always been dicks to some extent.

There was a farm, you see, in New Haven, Connecticut, USA. This farm was owned by a Wakeman family, and Mrs Wakeman oversaw the birth of a little piglet that had some fairly clear deformities.

For starters, it had a stunted snout, which gave it a slightly human appearance around the face... and it only had one eye. Such things were, at the time, considered to be omens of one kind or another, and word quickly spread of this one-eyed piglet with human features.

> *"...the head was most strange, it had one eye, in the bottom of the forehead, which was like a child's... a thing of flesh grew forth and hung down, it was hollow and like a man's instrument of generation. A nose, mouth and chin deformed but no much unlike a child's, the neck and ears also had such a resemblance..."*
> *- Records of the Colony and Plantation of New Haven, 1641*

Basically, a face like a child's, with one big eye, and a willy hanging off it like it had every right to be there. In this day and age we would call this an unfortunate genetic malady, and maybe consider not breeding from that sow again.

Back then, however...

Enter Mr George Spencer. Poor George Spencer only had one eye, having lost his to disease (or accident, the records aren't entirely clear) some years previously. He happened to live not too far from where the piglet was born, and it was assessed that he was therefore... suspicious... for having potentially had carnal relations with said sow to produce said piglet.

George wasn't just some one-eyed mendicant, either. He was a man of some means, because he had the money to afford himself a glass eye. I mean... I'm not saying that he *didn't* have carnal relations with the sow... but I am saying that there is no way in hell that this was going to result in the birth of a man/pig hybrid.

We know this now because... science. Back then...

> *"A strange impression was also upon many that saw the monster (guided by the near resemblance of the eye) that one George Spencer... had been an actor in unnatural and abominable filthiness with the sow. "*
> *- Records of the Colony and Plantation of New Haven, 1641*

So it came to pass that a pig with one eye, and a gentleman sausage on its face, was born... and the man who had one eye (but apparently no gentleman sausage on his face... at least, if there were, you'd expect the reports to mention it) was blamed because... well... one and one add up to twenty-seven, don't they?

George may have been able to acquire himself a glass eye, but he had been in some trouble with the law before. The New Haven leaders got together, had a bit of a discussion, and decided to arrest Mr Spencer for... abominable filthiness... and commit him for trial.

Witnesses at the trial were happy to testify that poor George was a habitual fibber, was often quite rude, periodically expressed disdain at holy days, and often failed to pray. It stood to reason then that he and Ms Sow were intimate in a way that only one man and his neighbour's pig could be:

- They knew each other in the biblical sense.
- They bumped uglies.
- They had a rousing game of sink the sausage.
- They played Thomas the Tank Engine at Paddington Station.

... even if this was a load of blinkered ignorance at a court *so* kangaroo that it was conducted by barristers on pogo sticks.[108]

Even though nobody saw the vile and depraved act... almost certainly because it didn't actually happen, let's be fair... poor George Spencer was convicted of bestiality, and hanged in April 1642.

EDWARD TEACH (1680-1718)

Pirates. Scourge of the high seas. When you think 'pirates' (and you aren't too invested in Disney movies) then the name that comes strikingly close to the top of the list is Blackbeard. That's the name - the title, almost- that was given to Edward Teach.

EARLY LIFE

Teach was probably not even his real name - and we will never know what was. Pirates - certainly those capable of rising up the ranks to captain their own ships - were not notorious because they were stupid... and would often assume a name to avoid bringing shame upon their families.

What becomes clear is that he was fairly well educated at least, able to read and write and calculate, and this suggests that he came from a fairly well-off background - given the nature of general education in the late 17th century.

If Teach had any family he cared about back

in England, chances are he would be using an assumed name.. and that's all we will likely know of early years. Before he took to the sea - most likely as a crewmember aboard a privateer, operating on behalf of Her Majesty's Government - history overlooks him.

PRIVATEER

It was a time of great strife for England. Her two long-time enemies France and Spain had formed an alliance and were carving their fortunes out of the Americas. England had a toehold in the West Indies - and of course a reasonable (though contested) portion of what is now the United States of America.

The privateers would prey on Spanish ships and Teach was described by 18th century historians as having "often distinguished himself for his uncommon boldness and personal courage."

As the war with Spain sputtered, Teach found himself without privateer employment, so took a position on one of the many pirate vessels operating out of Nassau - the closest the pirates ever had to a capital - on the island of New Providence.

PIRATE

Initially sticking to only Spanish targets, the profits were sparse, and the captain - Benjamin Hornigold - was voted off his ship and Teach took over as captain. Pirates, it turns out, were surprisingly democratic in nature.[109]

The willingness of Teach to commit acts of piracy against any target, and his success at doing so, drew attention. His tendency to fill his large black beard with lit fuses, and his ferocity in battle, earned him the nickname "Blackbeard" - and the legend grew.

Soon, taking a new flagship from the French and re-naming her "Queen Anne's Revenge". Surprisingly - while ferocious - there are no records at all of Blackbeard murdering any of those he took captive. Even the threat of attack by his ship was often enough to cause the rich merchantmen to strike their colours.

Teach would generally take only what they could carry, any men who wished to join him, and that would be that. The merchantmen were generally insured.

Amassing a fleet, Teach raided the islands, disrupted shipping, and evaded British and Spanish pirate hunters with surprising alacrity. Then, at the height of his power, and hubris, the fleet blockaded the port of Charles Town in the Province of South Carolina.

He made demands of the Governor for supplies, and ransacked every ship they were able to stop entering or exiting the port. All this under the threat of executing hostages... a state of affairs which fortunately never came to pass.

Ever the pragmatist, Teach was no stranger to the concept of grounding his ships or marooning his men if it would increase the share of treasure for the rest of them. You could always capture another ship, and men were a dime a dozen in the West Indies.

There were plenty of other adventures and battles, but ultimately, the pirate hunters caught up with him. Lieutenant Robert Maynard of HMS Pearl found Teach and his forces at anchor.

THE FINAL ASSAULT

Even denied the ability to manoeuvre, the battle against the pirates was devastating, and Maynard lost a third of his manpower in one single salvo from Teach. Maynard was cunning, however, and had many men hidden below decks, believing that Teach would succeed in boarding him.

It worked, and as Teach found himself on the verge of victory against the pirate hunters, dozens more men burst up from the holds, and the battle was renewed. Hand to hand fighting was vicious, but ultimately the pirates were defeated. As with the best narratives, Teach found himself facing Maynard himself on the bridge of Maynard's flagship.

While Maynard appeared more than willing to

have it all come down to a duel between captains, Maynard's men were having none of it, and they mobbed Teach and killed him where he stood. Maynard, upon examining Teach's body, recorded that the wounds he had taken were nothing short of shocking. Teach had been shot at least five times, and stabbed or cut more than twenty.

Teach's headless corpse was thrown unceremoniously into the sea, and his head affixed to the bow of Maynard's ship. Teach's head was eventually mounted on a spike at the entrance to Chesapeake Bay as a warning to other pirates, and it stood there for several years.

Amassing a fleet, Teach raided the islands, disrupted shipping, and evaded British and Spanish pirate hunters with surprising alacrity.

FREDERIC TUDOR (1783-1864)

If you were unfortunate enough to be bombarded with the movie 'Frozen' in the last decade, perhaps because you have a child of a certain age, then you will be more than passingly familiar with the opening sequence where a gang of singing men is cutting chunks of ice from a frozen lake. There's a good chance that they were working for someone like Frederic Tudor.

Ice was, quite simply, a remarkably valuable commodity... and Tudor was its king.

Born the third son of a Boston lawyer, Tudor launched into business at the remarkably young age of thirteen, having no interest in furthering his education. His trading travels took him to the Caribbean, which is – we can all agree – known for its general all-around hot weather.

He knew that the secret to great returns was to find something that the other fellow doesn't have, and then foster a need for it. Once the other fellow *needs* what you have, you sell it to him, and pocket the considerable profits. The Caribbean had no ice. Boston was often full of the stuff.

In 1806, Tudor was successful enough to afford his own ship. A brig called "Favourite", and within it he placed blocks of ice, cut from his family farm, and transported it over 1500 miles (2400km) to the Caribbean island of Martinique.

Now, the media of the time thought this whole escapade a ridiculous folly, and described it as "a slippery speculation"... but Tudor had planned ahead. He'd had family members travel ahead and secure exclusive rights to sell ice throughout the islands.

The problem was that ice, by its nature, was a bit melty... and the Caribbean islands were, by *their* nature, a bit warm. The first shipment of ice melted severely, and while Tudor did sell what remained, he ran at a loss of over $4,500 – a considerable sum at the time.

Several more shipments were met with the same loss. The ice was simply melting too fast. Add to this the betrayal of an agent resulting in the funds from his first actually profitable trip disappearing... and Tudor was in severe financial trouble. He actually spent two years in a debtor's prison.. but was able to borrow money to repay debts and buy more ice for another attempt.

Pursued for remaining debts, Tudor set sail againin 1815. His ice business was turning a profit now... but a disastrous attempt to transport fresh fruit in the other direction almost drove him under again.

The turning point was Tudor's experimentation with insulation. He eventually realised that if you packed the outer surfaces of the ice with sawdust and wood-shavings, the ice would melt at a much slower rate.

Over the following few years, Tudor's ice trade flourished. He even managed to transport over 100 tons of ice to India, and Calcutta soon became his most profitable destination, netting him over $200,000.

Tudor's ice trade had remarkable flow-on economic effects. It became possible to transport perishables further, expanded trade, and cemented his reputation as a remarkable visionary. By the 1840s, almost the entire world was able to receive shipments of ice... and while Tudor was at this time no longer the market leader, he was comfortably the leading light in a new global industry.

GERALD HUGH TYRWHITT-WILSON (1883-1950)

Every now and again there is someone who stands on the crossroads between Villainous and just plain Weird and stays there. I think Tyrwhitt-Wilson stands right in the middle of this crossroads and leans well over towards the road to Villainy.

Born in England in 1883, Tyrwhitt-Wilson was raised mainly by his grandmother, as his father (a Royal Navy officer) was frequently absent, and his mother had little inclination.

This doesn't really have much bearing on the tale, but it perhaps goes some way to explaining why he grew up so odd. His mother was described as "of small mind" and "extremely prejudiced", and his grandmother was a self-righteous religious zealot.

At the age of 35, he inherited a title (14th Baron Berners) and flipping great wodges[110] of money from a deceased uncle, and - while he was never destitute in his youth - it gave him a freedom he had never really experienced before.

It wasn't wealth that made him odd though... when quite young, he had thrown a pet dog out of an upstairs window to teach it to fly... something it turned out the dog was not really cut out for.

As an adult, he would capture pigeons around his estate and dye them vibrant colours before releasing them again. When a noted lady travel-writer visited him, he treated the lady's horse to a tea party.

His garden was made largely of paper flowers, and he erected signs all over his estate, noting things like "Mangling done here!" (in the garden) or "Prepare to meet thy God" (inside a wardrobe).

All innocuous stuff, really... but it didn't end there. He would drive around the nearby villages in his Rolls-Royce wearing a pigs-head mask, in order to scare the locals. When he wasn't scaring them, he would drive past simultaneously playing his clavichord.

He hated public transport, but would sometimes travel to London by train. He would make sure that he was the only person in a compartment by wearing a black skull-cap, dark glasses, and leering at people out of the window, creepily inviting them to join him for "fun times".

When someone was foolish enough to accept his offer, he would produce a large rectal thermometer, which he would suck on while making all manner of outlandish noises, in order to encourage them to leave.[111] [112]

He managed to offend several his peers with his publication of "The Girls of Radcliff Hall", a book in which he portrayed peers and colleagues as students in a girls' school - which he published under a pseudonym.

The initial run is believed to have been purchased in bulk by one of the people he pilloried in the tale - and destroyed en masse. It did go on to be republished, however.

Regardless of his bizarre behaviour, he was a popular fellow, and he had many famous visitors, such as composer Igor Stravinsky, artist Salvador Dali, and writer H. G. Wells. He was a notable author of mainly humorous work, as well as a composer and artist.

He died in 1950 at the age of 66, having proven himself a whimsical rogue, leaving his estate to his estranged lover, and a legacy of hijinks behind him.

THE VAN BUREN SISTERS (1916)

In 1916, Augusta and Adeline Van Buren completed a 5,500 mile (8,851km) journey across the continental United States on separate motorcycles. They were also arrested multiple times for their villainous perfidy.

They had to contend with appalling roads, sometimes mountainous terrain, some remarkably unseasonal bad weather, and plenty of other issues... but they completed the trip, making them the second and third women respectively to cross the continental United States on motorcycles.

They were also the first women to reach 14,109-foot summit of Colorado's Pikes Peak by any motor vehicle. But they were, nevertheless, considered villains. Why was this?

Had they stolen the motorcycles?

No. Their twin 1,000cc Indian Power Plus

motorcycles (equipped with gas headlights) were legitimately purchased from the Indian Motorcycle Company. Back in 1916, these were *the* motorcycles to have, and they ran to an exorbitant US$275 each in the day. That's roughly US$7,000 in today's money. The sisters were not short of a dollar or two, as they were descendants of a former US President, and came from a wealthy family.

Did they cause mayhem along the route?

They certainly attracted attention, and they certainly committed crimes... but not in the way that you might think. There was no mayhem in the traditional sense. No bank robberies, no drive-by shootings, no burnouts outside the Police station. They did have to be rescued once, after becoming lost in the desert, but that involved the inconvenience of only one chap who was able to guide them back to a road... not a huge call-out on the tax-payer's dime.

Were they trying to promote anarchy or rebellion?

No. There were no anti-government slogans, no "What are you rebelling against? What've you got?" showdowns. In fact, if anything, they were trying to be especially patriotic.

They were part of a 'preparedness' organisation and wanted to show that women could be a productive part of the US war effort - as the US was steaming quickly towards entering World War I - and demonstrate that women could help to shoulder the burden of sacrifice for their country, even if they weren't allowed to fight. Specifically, they wanted to show that women could become dispatch riders on the frontlines, able to travel long distances quickly and efficiently.

So, why were they constantly being arrested? They were wearing trousers.

That's it. Just that. They were wearing trousers.

I don't mean that they should have been riding around with no pants on[113], but that even as late as 1916 there were expected dress codes, and women could be arrested for wearing men's clothes.

As the Van Buren sisters were wearing leather riding gear - including trousers and jackets - this was considered a ghastly breach of etiquette, not to mention the law, and couldn't be overlooked by... well, by the less-evolved members of society.

According to the law, they should have been crossing the continental United States wearing dresses or skirts, and (probably) riding sidesaddle... and according to media of the day, they were "using the national preparedness issue as an excellent excuse to escape their roles as housewives."

Ultimately the sister's petition to be allowed to become dispatch riders was denied.

They each had successful later lives, however. Augusta went on to become a pilot, and Adeline became a lawyer.

In 2002, these remarkable sisters were inducted into the American Motorcyclist Association's Motorcycle Hall of Fame... but their epic journey - which would almost be a doddle with today's technology - and the ridiculous social barriers that they faced certainly deserves a wider audience.

ANTONIE VAN LEEUWENHOEK (1632-1723)

These days we'd treat a brainiac like van Leeuwenhoek with a little more respect, one hopes... but for someone who is considered the father of modern microbiology, rather a lot of people thought he was a nutter or a charlatan at the time.

To be clear, I'm not saying van Leeuwenhoek himself was any kind of problem, so much as his image at the time, and who people thought he was. Oh, he had his skeletons in cupboards, same as everyone, but ultimately, he was just a guy living in a tough world who found out some startling stuff before anyone was ready to believe it.

Let's start with the *theory of spontaneous generation*. Back in the 17th century, people thought that the 'lower life forms' such as fleas just popped into existence. Earthworms, for example, many thought were the result of cast-off horse hairs marinating in the right kind of puddle.

While I can see this as a logical step on the road to understanding, you'd think that someone would try soaking some horsehair in a puddle to watch the wormification process. Apparently, they did not. As for the instantaneous generation of fleas... all I can say is thank goodness the same thing wasn't true for elephants.

So, when someone like van Leeuwenhoek comes up and says "actually, I've seen fleas having sexy-times" people tended to raise an eyebrow and take a few cautious steps backwards.[114]

Born in Holland, van Leeuwenhoek started off as a draper, running his own shop, and he started making microscopes as a side-effect of building up an interest in lens making.[115]

His early life was fairly tragic. He lost four children and his wife by the age of 34. His childhood years were spent bouncing around due to the death of both father and stepfather, before ending up with an uncle who taught him the trade of drapery.

His first microscopes - basically just lenses - were made to help him see smaller and finer threads in greater detail. From such small needs to great discoveries come.

Van Leeuwenhoek went on to discover:

- Bacteria
- Infusoria (freshwater microscopic life)
- Small bits of cells
- Spermatozoa (don't tell me you wouldn't try it!)
- Individual strands of muscle

So, why was he vilified at the time of his discoveries, even though he went on to reap huge rewards from scientific institutions? Some of it was because of sheer jealousy. The draper, rather than the scientist, making ground-breaking announcements about the nature of the world? Unheard of!

He was, after all, an amateur scientist. He was still working as a draper and a lensmaker at the time. The fact that he kept much of his lensmaking techniques top secret likely didn't help matters. He had developed a rather clever method using droplets of molten glass, rather than grinding, to produce very high-magnification lenses. He didn't want to share.

His responses to his detractors were considered, and generally backed up with fact. He rarely resorted to the baser arguments that heated his opponent's words.

Whereas I suffer many contradictions,

> *and oft-times hear it said that I do but tell fairy tales about the little animals, and that there are people in France who do not scruple to say that those are not living creatures which I exhibit, ... I make bold to say, that people who say such things have not yet advanced so far as to be able to carry out good observations.*
> *- Antonie van Leeuwenhoek (1680)*

The Royal Society upon hearing about van Leeuwenhoek's descriptions of bacteria, for example, mostly scoffed. None of their microscopes were powerful enough. Van Leeuwenhoek had to obtain affidavits from prominent citizens of his town to attest to the fact that he was not a looney, and not given to making things up.

It took a while, but eventually the Royal Society developed a powerful enough microscope, saw the bacteria for themselves, and welcomed van Leeuwenhoek with open arms... publishing several of his earlier submissions - which had been held in abeyance, as they were considered far too unlikely to be true.

The Royal Society - perhaps chagrined by their earlier scoffing - presented the microbiologist with a handsome coat of arms on a silver case.

So, the villainy isn't van Leeuwenhoek. Nor was it James Lind, or Ignaz Semmelweis, or Galileo Galilei, or any number of remarkable visionaries who gave us knowledge and common sense. It's the people who laughed at them, or just disbelieved them without any good reason other than classism, racism, sexism, or ego. It's still going on today, and we need to do better.

JAN JANSZOON VAN HAARLEM (1570-1641)

Calling someone a Barbary Pirate brings up visions of derring-do, and pitched battles on heaving ships on the high seas... but a Barbary Pirate is just a pirate who operated out of North Africa, mainly during the 17th century.

Jan Janszoon van Haarlem (1575-1641) was such a pirate, originally Dutch, but operating out of Algeria and Morocco.

He had started his career as a privateer for the Dutch, with permission to harass Spanish shipping. It didn't take long to decide that looting Spanish ships wasn't enough for him, and working for the Dutch was limiting his success as a scoundrel, so he decided that anyone would be fair game... and now he was in it for himself.

During his reign as a pirate, he helped found the city state of *Salé* in North Africa, and operated as its first president, and grand admiral.

Salé was pretty short-lived. It was a brutal place, and its principle economic foundation was slavery and piracy, so you can imagine that people who didn't like (a) enslavement, and (b) being pillaged, would jump on it pretty hard as soon as they could.

However, founding Salé meant that he changed from Scourge of the High Seas to Administrator to the various Scourges of the High Seas, and he'd get so bored that occasionally he'd have his lads load up a ship, and he'd womble off for a few months to try his luck at piracy once more.

Once he sailed all the way to Iceland - partly because he'd never been there before, and partly chasing tales of rich cargoes, but even after raiding the fishing village of Grindavík, they came away with little more than some dried fish and a few fisherman slaves.

His most famous raid was in Ireland, and the town of Baltimore. The reason the town was chosen was because one of his crew was a Roman Catholic Irishman, and when he heard of his captain's intentions, directed him to a Protestant town, well away from his home town.

The raid was quick and thorough. There wasn't

much in the way of loot, but the pirates captured 108 slaves from Ireland, and took them back to North Africa for sale.[116]

According to the Icelandic prisoners at least, the captives were treated more-or-less humanely (apart from the whole being sold into slavery thing, of course) though few ever returned home to tell the tales.

It didn't all go well for Jan Janszoon, however. In 1635, while sailing past the coast of Tunisia, he was attacked by Knights Hospitaller - also known as The Knights Malta.[117] He was taken to Malta's dungeons and tortured there. He remained in the dark for almost five years, and his health suffered significantly as a result.

He wasn't without his friends, however, and upon learning of his capture, his ongoing survival, and his whereabouts, a massive corsair raid was staged to rescue him and the few surviving members of his crew.

His capture and imprisonment had unfortunately ruined his health, and he was described by one of his offspring as having become a feeble old man within those five years. He retired into obscurity and is believed to have died a year or two later.

FRIEDRICH WILHELM VOIGT (1849-1922)

Voigt was a wrong-un. Born in Prussia in 1849, his early life was filled with criminal enterprise. This is the short tale of a long-term villain who made quite the mark. 'scuse pun.

Voigt first saw the inside of a prison cell at age 14, after he had been arrested for petty theft. It was only fourteen days incarceration, perhaps intended to set an example and scare him straight, but it certainly didn't work.

In his 27 years between the ages of 15 and 42, he spent 25 of them in prison for a variety of offending, including theft, burglary, and forgery. If you had it, he'd steal it, or copy it.

Rehabilitation was not really a thing back in 19th century Prussia... so he was likely destined to continue to offend, because it was all he knew by that point of his life.

Voigt was probably quite lucky, however, because forgery was often punishable by death in 1800s Prussia. The prisons in Prussia were horrible, but even worse, he could easily have been transported to Siberia... which would have been almost certain doom.

He was released from prison in the Winter of 1906 and left to fend mostly for himself. He drifted for a while but was genuinely trying to make good. He moved to Berlin and got a job working for a shoemaker.

He was never going to be a model citizen, but what happened next was eminently unfair... even though gainfully employed, and not committing any offences, local Police found out that he was an ex-convict and expelled him from the city as an 'undesirable'.

Catch-22. If you're a criminal in 19th Century Berlin, you're not allowed to work. If you're not allowed to work, you have little option but to turn to crime. The local constabulary were really not helping themselves here.

So, Voigt lost his job, and with little else to fall back on, it didn't take too long before he turned to crime again... but this time, his methods were a little less... usual. Ten days after being kicked out of the city, he returned and cobbled together parts of an army officer's uniform from different army-surplus shops. He gave himself the rank of captain and went forth to cause mayhem.

He set out for Köpenick, not far from Berlin, and on the way, he visited an army barracks and ordered four grenadiers, a sergeant, and six other soldiers to follow him.

With his men in tow, he ordered them to guard the city hall's exits, allowing nobody in or out. He gathered the local Police and had them scattered far and wide seeking out non-existent trouble. He posted a guard on the local post office to allow no communication in or out for a set period of time.

Then he had Köpenick's treasurer von Wiltberg, and mayor Georg Langerhans arrested and detained, citing charges of corruption. This was of course, all complete nonsense, and while his duped army was frantically going about its business, Voigt took the opportunity to relieve the treasury of 4002 marks and 37 pfennigs.

My maths is pretty appalling at the best of times, but based on 1906 currency, and calculating for inflation to modern era, this probably works out to somewhere in the region of USD$120,000.

He then told his men to take the treasurer and mayor to Berlin for interrogation, and skipped town on the train, after a sneaky change of clothes. It could have been the perfect crime, if Voigt hadn't been a bit of an idiot.

You see, he'd concocted the plan while he was imprisoned previously, and while he had never seriously intended to go through with it, his unemployment gave him little option. The problem is that he'd also told a cellmate... and that cellmate, recognising the modus operandi from the newspaper, dobbed him in immediately in the hope of a reward. No honour among thieves.

Voigt was arrested only ten days after the heist and sentenced to another four years in prison for forgery, impersonating an officer, and wrongful imprisonment. He had captured the public's attention, however, and had become a global sensation. His heist was reported far and wide, including an illustrated article in the popular British Illustrated Police News.

So popular was he, in fact, that Kaiser Wilhelm II pardoned him only two years later in 1908... and Voigt was again a free man.

Now though, he was able to capitalise on his fame. He toured Dresden, Vienna and Budapest in variety shows, restaurants and amusement parks. He made money signing pictures and autographs. He starred in plays depicting his own exploits. He published a book titled *How I became the Captain of Köpenick*.

He even went on tour in America... though he had to sneak in via Canada due to being unable to obtain a visa.

In 1910, he moved to Luxembourg with a good pension provided by a rich dowager. He purchased a house and retired. Voigt died in Luxembourg in 1922.

MANFRED VON RICHTOFEN (1892-1918)

Famously joining the Imperial German Army Air Service from the Supply Branch with his written application containing the phrase "I have not gone to war in order to collect cheese and eggs", Manfred von Richtofen grew to become one of the most recognised and celebrated names in military history.

Born into a noble family, a Freiherr (loosely translated as 'Baron') in 1892, in what is now Poland, Manfred became an enthusiastic hunter and rider. When World War I broke out in 1914, he signed up as a cavalryman.

The cavalry was the domain of the nobility, and the world had moved on to the point where cavalry was largely obsolete. Manfred was consigned to reconnaissance riding until the warring nations resorted to trench warfare. At which point, there was little need for cavalry.

He therefore found himself - a Baron whose family prided itself on martial excellence - riding dispatch, until electronic communication took over, and he was further relegated to the Supply Branch, in charge of - as he put it - collecting cheese and eggs.

Far from the fighting, and no job at all for a nobleman.

One fateful day, he had the opportunity to see one of the new German fighter aircraft at close hand and applied to join the Imperial German Air Service - *Die Fliegertruppen des deutschen Kaiserreiches* - which later became *Die Luftstreitkräfte*.

At the time, it was considered quite a logical step for a cavalryman to become a fighter pilot. For starters, there were a lot of them, and they weren't really needed as cavalrymen anymore... and secondly, they tended to be "the right sort" of person. That is... educated, and much as I hate to say it, from the correct end of the demographic pool. Wealthy nobility.

This wasn't just Germany. Many of the early Allied fighter pilots came from similar backgrounds, and it was only the pressing need for more and more pilots that resulted in 'standards being lowered' to allow pretty much anyone in.

At first, he had a slow start. A few accidents, and some trouble controlling his aircraft made it look like he was not a natural flyer... but he soon came to grips with the machine and - under the tutelage of the ace pilot *Oswald Boelcke* - soon began to understand how things were done.

His first 'kill' was 26 April 1916, wherein he shot down a French fighter over allied lines. He was not officially credited with the victory as it could not be verified independently. He did go on to rack up many victories in the air, was promoted to lead Jasta 11 flying squadron. Not long after this he was flying in the bright red triplane that earned him his name 'The Red Baron'.

His sixteenth victory in the air earned him the *Pour le Mérite*, or Blue Max, which was the highest decoration awarded by the German armed forces at the time.

For every victory in the air, Richthofen would commission a small silver cup, engraved with the date and the type of aircraft he had shot down. He discontinued this practice after silver became too hard to acquire.

Only a few months after his Blue Max, he experienced a traumatic head-wound and was shot down by a formation of comparatively primitive British F.E.2D two-seater aircraft. He barely managed to survive the plunge from the sky, got his plane under control, and crash landed in a field behind his own lines. He spent months in convalescence and had multiple operations to remove bone fragments from the skull wound. He was never again able to fly without nausea and headaches.

Nevertheless, he racked up a total of eighty kills in his brief career, and upon returning to action found that the allied aircraft had very-much caught up with the German technology.

On 21 April 1918 - Pursuing a Sopwith Camel at low altitude over the trenches, it is believed that Richthofen was likely shot through the chest by anti-aircraft fire, killing him almost instantly. There was some controversy about this, as he was under fire from at least one aircraft and several ground units at the time.

His plane climbed, stalled, and crashed into the ground behind Allied lines. The first soldiers on the scene found Richthofen already dead, and the aircraft was quickly dismantled for souvenirs.

Unlike his aircraft, Richthofen's body was treated with great respect, and he received a funeral with full military honours conducted by the personnel of No. 3 Squadron Australian Flying Corps. He was later re-interred in 1922 and received a state funeral.

Throughout his career, and as his legend grew, Richthofen became increasingly aware of the attempt to use him as a patriotic propaganda-piece. While he was certainly patriotic, he didn't particularly like the idea of his name being used in this manner, though he didn't noticeably shy away from public adulation.

It was a different age. War graduating into Total War as the last bitter shreds of chivalry blew, tattered, into the mud. Nevertheless, The Red Baron passed into legend. He has become something of a pop-culture icon, with games named after him, books written about him, even gaining a tongue-in-cheek rival in the dog Snoopy from the popular cartoon series Peanuts.

I'm not sure what he would have thought about that.

REMARKABLE PEOPLE

His sixteenth victory in the air earned him the Pour le Mérite, or Blue Max, which was the highest decoration awarded by the German armed forces at the time.

AFTERWORD

If you've made it this far, and come to the end of the book, then I applaud your perseverance. Imagine a loud *"DING!"* and bright floaty letters proudly proclaiming "Achievement Unlocked". You are now well prepared for the test.

If you've just jumped straight to this bit... that's a bit weird.

But I guess if you're still reading then you'll want to know a little bit about me. I'm fairly resigned to the fact that I'm unlikely to retire on the proceeds of my writing... but I enjoy the process, so I guess I'll keep going.

I live in New Zealand, which is a pretty little country quite frequently left of maps, to the right-hand side of Australia. I have a wife, a small child, and two kittens. More or less in that order, depending on who is demanding most of my attention at the time. I wasn't born in New Zealand... I'm Welsh. Having arrived here before turning two years old, I can reliably inform you that I've lost most of my Welsh accent.

I also run a Facebook group called ***Villainy***

(with four other very helpful volunteers) where most of the content for the books gets its first experimental airing before being compiled into book form. I can refine it there, you see, and test it across multiple groups before deciding whether I should give it a tweak or two:

http://www.facebook.com/groups/TopVillains

Thank you for buying my book. Whether it's on Kindle, or made of actual dead trees, I appreciate it, and define my self-worth by how much you enjoy it. Feel free to drop me a note at:

villainybooks@mordorbbs.com

Rob Mordor
New Zealand
January 2023

---

[1] I'm not really clear on the intended pronunciation here. Is it supposed to be pronounced like "Dennis", or like "P-"... never mind. Either way, it doesn't seem like a very kingly name. Kings are all called John or Charles or something. Dennis is the guy who you'd send your Ford Cortina to for an oil change.

[2] I'll have to remember that. Could be a great thing to request on a birthday cake.

[3] Little Nero was called Lucius initially, until adopted by Emperor Claudius some years later, but that's just confusing, so I'll refer to him as Nero throughout. Trying to trace Roman familial links is like trying to

work out which strand of spaghetti is going where, and then realising all of them are multi-ended.

[4] I can imagine this being said with a self-deprecating little chuckle, and it is probably just as well he never lived to see how his lad turned out, because he certainly wasn't "good for the state or the people".

[5] Your very bones, I say!

[6] If you're Scottish, then some of those names might mean something to you. They go a little over my head, quite frankly, and may as well just be little sound loops of Paul McCartney singing "Mull of Kintyre" at me while eating a bagpipe.

... actually, is it possible to have a single bagpipe? Or are bagpipes always plural in nature? I'm guessing there's one bag with several pipes, but if you unscrewed one of those, would it be a single bagpipe, or just a pipe, if it's not connected to the bag? This is going to annoy me now.

Come to think of it, is 'haggis' both singular and plural? Is it one haggis, many haggis? Haggises? Haggi? Issues like this are a good reason why nobody has ever properly conquered Scotland. I mean, sure, England probably thought they did, but I suspect they mainly spent their time wandering around confused, mulling their kintyres and girvanning their ballantraes.

[7] I suppose I am pretty sure haggis is both plural and singular. Like sheep. Which would make some kind of logical sense, as one of the primary ingredients of haggis is sheep.

Actually, are a bagpipe made of sheeps?

[8] In short, one of those people who used to be described as "your betters", when you knew damn well that there was no 'better' about it. It's people like Beresford who make me genuinely wonder why England didn't face the same gentry-ending ructions that gripped France not all that many years beforehand.

[9] Give a young lad a dollar and he'll buy some sweets and watch some telly. Give a young lad a million dollars, and he'll wrap his sports car around a lamp-post and set fire to a stadium.

[10] They were still technically transporting criminals to Australia in the 1850s. You can pretty-much guarantee that anyone who wasn't the son of a wealthy landowner, and a marquess in his own right, would've been a bit worried about sourcing a lifetime supply of crocodile repellent at this point.

[11] But probably not at the same time. While you can certainly put quill to parchment on horseback, all that up-and-down movement at even a moderate canter would make anything you wrote quite illegible. Also, you were probably at risk of impaling yourself on your quill... which would make all the other knights laugh at you. Pride was everything back in the 1500s.

[12] Hehe.

[13] Look... loyalty was clearly not one of Blood's strong points. I mean, sure, the changing political climate of England in the 1600s meant that you had to adapt

pretty quickly, but 'enlightened self-interest' seems to have held a special candle for Blood at this point.

[14] Association of Democratic Monarchists Representing All Women - - which, stop me if I'm wrong - actually has the acronym ADMRAW... but then I'm not a politician.

[15] I have real trouble with this idea. It would be like a modern bank-robber having a get-away bicycle. I suppose such things *do* happen. Just the idea of a fairly diminutive, if sprightly, fellow – weighed down by a bag of gold – running like hell from a fusillade of six-gun fire after robbing a stagecoach, makes me rather more admiring of the man than I probably should be.

[16] I said he left poetry. I didn't say it was *good* poetry.

[17] In one case, it was noted that the poetry was too good to have been Boles.

[18] Note to self: Research haiku rickshaw robberies on the Japanese mainland from 1888 onwards.

[19] It was still a big one, but probably not as satisfying as one that was uncut.

[20] And yes... I am aware of the irony of using '**' in place of 'uc' in the above quote... but needs must as my editor glares at me over the top of her terrifying glasses.

[21] In the same way a small child make make excited "pew pew!" noises when drawing some action-scene with crayons and a crumpled piece of paper, you can imagine me muttering darkly as I type. It's cathartic. You should try it.

[22] A polar bear would eat a Great Auk like popcorn. They've never eaten a penguin though. Their claws aren't long enough.

[23] It is from here that we get the word "awkward", the embarrassment one feels upon being whipped for inconveniencing a protected sea-bird.

[24] That's a lie. I made that up. Damn, but I wish it were true.

[25] Not to be confused with 'naturists'. It was far too cold for that sort of carry-on.

[26] There are willies in it.

[27] If I'm honest, the phrase "daring armed raid" and "probably drunken singing" don't usually go well together, and this is the case here too. You don't hear of cat burglars stopping to sing a couple of bawdy rugby songs while they're trying to remove a statue from The Louvre. Not good ones, anyway.

[28] You might think that this is a lot harder to do tens of thousands of years after the fact than it might be when the hyenas were still living there... but realising that there are *still* prehistoric hyena living in a cave would generally have been met by quickly realising that they were *quite* hungry... and that they were really surprisingly zippy for such large animals.

[29] Somehow, the idea had reached the lawmakers that being poor was a moral failing, and not only could you end up in prison, but they would *charge you* for being there... and if you couldn't afford to repay, they'd just keep you in. It was a Catch-22 situation. There are people who had been in prison for decades after simply

being unable to pay a bill.

[30] In this particular instance, the phrase "If the shoes fits..." springs immediately to mind.

[31] The phrase "professional business" perhaps doesn't clarify things in this example. Let's say that he was there to engage his medical skills, rather than his marital ones.

[32] Who the hell buys a gold organ? I mean, having so much money that you don't know what to do with is one thing... but using it to buy something so obviously pointless is... (sigh) ... basic human nature. I've answered my own question. Carry on.

[33] Though how he noticed his wife playing a gold organ without asking a few questions is something that should potentially have been explored further.

[34] Not so much in mine, alas.

[35] Treatments for mental illness in the 14th century included such things as having holes drilled in your head, eating the genitalia of various small mammals, and overdosing people with emetics and laxatives, so you could choose whether to crap yourself to health, or vomit your way to a brighter future. All horrifically barbaric stuff.

[36] I don't know if you've ever accidentally glued your thighs to your elbows, but it's not a dignified or elegant way to spend a Friday night. Trust me.

[37] Also, the Welsh longbows would have still been a tough nut to crack. Not that I'm holding up an awesome flag with a dragon on it or anything.

Gwlad, Gwlad, pleidiol wyf i'm gwlad,
Tra môr yn fur i'r bur hoff bau,
O bydded i'r heniaith barhau.

[38] I can only imagine the sheer relief about the court.

[39] In all fairness though, if you're a fan of history, "A period of instability" should be the tagline for France... which has likely seen more warp-and-weft than just about any other nation in the West.

[40] Not at the same time – though that's something I would pay to watch.

[41] Commanded *by Capt. Wichard von Alvensleben*, the regular German troops surrounded the SS forces. So intimidated were they by the overwhelming number of regular troops, the SS forces simply drove away and left everyone behind.

[42] These days, if your neighbour has a nice house and a pretty garden, you might sigh wistfully and wish you had a nice house and a pretty garden. Back in the 1300s, you'd sharpen your favourite pointy stick, and pop over for a ~~stab~~ chat.

[43] If you want a confession, torture is the way to go. It is not the way to go if you want the truth. After a certain point, you will admit to pretty-much anything they want you to, just to get them to turn off the Justin Bieber music.

[44] You don't get better names for fleets and flagships than that. Heck, if she wasn't running up the Jolly Roger and shouting the French equivalent of "Avast, ye scurvy lubbers!" I will be very disappointed.

[45] I'm going to take a moment here to just sort-of facepalm quietly to myself. Feel free to do the same.

[46] Though, in all fairness, I think I would quite like a pet ocelot.

[47] The undeniable fact that Charles XII was quite dead at the time, and had been for at least a decade, no doubt added some level of difficulty to the ruse.

[48] They didn't have television back then. A goat is the animal equivalent of a cheap sitcom. If you want drama you go for a Guinea Pig. Those guys can make quite the fuss if their lettuce happens to be a bit wilty.

[49] Which I was woefully disappointed to find out had absolutely nothing to do with ducks.

[50] I'm not entirely sure why they thought there was one... but when the King says something is a scourge, you generally have to take it as read that it's a scourge, and now it's *your* problem to fix.

[51] The "untwisted the top of the salt" or "put cling-film over the toilet bowl" sort of person makes me itch. I can't help but feel that there's a shallow grave somewhere which could be made useful by dint of a hastily utilised cricket-bat, and a rolled-up carpet.

[52] Based on this alone, if only he had been born 100 years later, we could have been the best of friends.

[53] Antihistamine and Hydrocortisone would absolutely tell you that your view of the universe was flawed, and how you should come to their night-classes and learn how to be a more responsible human.

[54] If you've never seen a Viking scarper, I recommend

it.

[55] Not to be confused with "Lorde", who lived a lot later, and is neither a Viking, nor particularly sailboat as far as I am aware.

[56] Though, ironically, they were invented by Scotsman Alexander Flemming over a thousand years later.

[57] I used to have rather the opposite problem. I always scored rather poorly in maths exams, and after my parents had spent a small fortune on tutors and extra study, I couldn't explain how I *didn't* know things.

[58] Who, it should be stressed, was not there at the time.

[59] I'm paraphrasing. I'm sure that not only was his *actual* phrasing rather more elegant and eloquent... but probably also in French.

[60] I'll admit that this confused me for a moment until I looked up 'coquette' and realised that it wasn't a small ball of crispy fried mashed potato. For future reference, that's a *croquette*. It is a small but notable distinction.

[61] In Barcelona in the early 1900s, it is *entirely* possible that both of these careers could have occurred in the same premises.

[62] For example, he had German forces in the Atlantic searching for non-existent convoys, which almost certainly saved real ships from real harm.

[63] Ptooi!

[64] !!!

[65] When I was 17 years of age, I was teaching myself computer coding, and drinking far too much soft-drink.

[66] I just get banished to another room. Occasionally hit with a pillow. Though waterboarding has been suggested. I don't think I snore at all. Certainly, I've never noticed it myself.

[67] Though there was potentially some argument about whether Hardin had counted to the full 'one hundred' before shouting "Coming! Ready or not!"

[68] Why do scientists sometimes conduct experiments on lawyers? There are some things even a rat wouldn't do.

[69] This involves running around with your arms outstretched shouting "VROOOOOM!" and "dakkadakkadakka!!!" and so on. It's not very elegant, and quite lacking in dignity. It was quite big on playgrounds in the early 1980s.

[70] As an aside, for those Terry Pratchett fans who have read down this far and are familiar with the rather excellent Night Watch book, the Roundworld Battle of Cable Street was a series of clashes in London, October 1936, between Oswald Mosley's fascist blackshirts, and various anti-fascist demonstrators.

[71] This peaked in 1858 with "The Great Stink"... but we're ahead of ourselves. It's a fascinating point in history, however, and one of the great engineering marvels of the age. Well worth some reading.

[72] There was a tendency for the Welsh to rebel against

John's rule... because of taxes, for example.

[73] Or "Typique" or something, at least.

[74] I'm not sure why this is a theme, really. I guess if you're a wealthy noble you're "eccentric", and if you're a poor coal miner you're "a nutter", and more likely to be locked up.

[75] Nothing quite unites the world like a good "I reckon", and a total lack of evidence to back it up. Significant amounts of money was being spent on pseudoscientific claptrap by the Royal Navy at this period in history.

[76] I guarantee that anyone who used to read Viz magazine back in the 1980s will *absolutely* have a certain character in mind at this point.

[77] I would say "there's your starter for ten right there", but I have family in the legal profession, and given that I damn well expect them to buy this bloody book, so that I can at least say *someone* has, chances are I'd never sell them another one if they saw me taking such a cheap shot at lawyers.

[78] It is amusing to note that Soper described his actions as "as diplomatic as possible". One wonders.

[79] For our American friends, this particular idiom means that he had a bit of money. Not that he couldn't keep track of his Roberts.

[80] Probably while facepalming and gritting his teeth.

[81] Which is a bit like saying the sea is a bit wet, or mountains are ever-so-slightly up-and-downy.

[82] Who were already not having an easy time of it, let's be fair.

[83] If decades of tactical and strategic turn-based gaming has taught me anything, it is that buying something is no guarantee that you'll be good at it. If the development of mankind had been coordinated by me as well as I coordinated it in a long list of computer games and simulations, we'd all still be living in trees and throwing sharp pieces of squirrel at each other.

[84] Foxes are a nuisance in today's world, but are generally skittish, and it's an unlucky person who's going to find themselves on the receiving end of a fox-bite. Either way, I think I'd rather be comfortable in the knowledge that any suitably motivated fox is going to have to bite through several layers of clothes before getting to my gentleman-sausage. Hunting does not appeal... and hunting in the buff appeals even less.

[85] A bridge seems to be such an unusually specific place to meet an attractive young lady. I suppose if you're absolutely dripping in money, it's easy enough to meet attractive young ladies on bridges. As an aside to any attractive young lady readers... why the fascination with bridges?

[86] Honestly, in 2023, this could probably describe quite a few of us.

[87] I have a sort-of fond mental image of this, all sped up, to the sound of "Yakety Sax". Occasionally, the mercenaries would stop and pat a little bald man on the head. You probably have to be from the United

Kingdom, and of a certain age, to appreciate this image.

[88] Let us add to this that Henson was black, and Peary was white, and that this was the early 1900s. Whenever I say something like "Peary was not a nice man", assume I am understating it considerably.

[89] Hehe.

[90] This sounds suspiciously like my time at university... only without the inherited titles, or the wealthy friends. Hands up everybody who's triggered right now.

[91] I thought the whole point of working as a waiter was to slip your screenplay into the hands of some unsuspecting producer... but perhaps that's just how it's shown on TV.

[92] Not to be confused with 'barista'. I know one barrister who was asked by a young lady what he did for a living at a party one evening, and when he told her, she said, "Ooh, nice. I love coffee."

[93] The worst I've ever encountered in a previous role was when someone threw someone else over a photocopier for some imagined slight or other. I always thought it odd that the person who was thrown got fired, and not the thrower - though I never did hear the full story. Back then photocopiers were about the size of Volkswagens, so it was quite the chuck.

[94] I don't mean he spent his retirement gadding about in warm water. Bath is a small city almost 100 miles

west of London. Named after the Roman baths that it was quite famous for back in the early days.

[95] A position which largely involved him shouting or telling the boy to get better. The odd thing is that it was working well enough that he remained in favour. If you don't buy into the whole 'healing power' thing (which I do not) then it's clear that this guy was either delusional, or a horrible cynical manipulator.

[96] Bodies go splish. Even onomatopoeia takes a back seat to propriety. Known scientific fact.

[97] It was also photographed, because evidence of his death was deemed fairly high priority. The photograph is easy to find, and public domain on the internet, but I wouldn't recommend looking it up.

[98] By way of context, find yourself a large hammer, and a sturdy tabletop. Put the thumb of your left hand on the tabletop. This represents the 21st company. Take the hammer in your right hand and raise it above your shoulder. This represents the German machinegun position. This is basically a practical demonstration of World War One tactics... where the plan was basically to keep throwing thumbs at the enemy until your other hand is too tired and covered with goo to hit them with the hammer.

[99] So... using the previous example... before putting your thumb on the sturdy tabletop the first time, jam it in a kitchen drawer.

[100] ... and use a heavier hammer.

[101] If it occurs to you that you should *stop* hitting your thumb with the hammer, start kicking yourself

in the ankle until you change your mind. The whole situation was basically this ridiculous.

[102] Emo much? Probably used to write teen angst haiku and wear black eyeline too... well, around one eye at least... but each to their own.

[103] I can't fault this, I suppose. There's supposed to be this whole honourable thing about being the bigger man, and letting go of slights of the past, but honestly, were I made emperor, I've got a list. I certainly wouldn't have people executed... but there'd be a few folk walking around who were legally required to wear clown-shoes, with "I'm stupid" tattooed on their foreheads.

[104] That is, until the noble families saw poor little Barry Chen working his new land and sent some of their larger friends over to have a quick word with him about re-settlement, and how nice the weather is in Cairo just at the moment.

[105] Pro Tip: Never discuss your plans for world domination in front of your ladies in waiting.

[106] You don't want to meet people who defecate in an *unusual* manner. This is the subject of many a TV show with names like "Embarrassing Bodies" or "Creatures from the Pit". It invariably ends either... badly... or with the entire world knowing that you poo funny. (Which is just another way of saying 'badly', if I think about it.)

[107] This is a special kind of horrible, when you think

about it.

[108] I can't help but think that the legal system would be improved remarkably if the legal representatives of both sides were required to use pogo sticks at all stages of deliberation.

[109] I would have to say that of all the things that surprised me about pirates, it was that the captaincy of any particular ship was decided by democratic process. If you were making them happy, you got to keep your job. I would imagine that the process of 'uncaptaining' a vessel would have been somewhat unfortunately abrupt.

[110] A wodge is a perfectly acceptable way of measuring cash. It loosely translates to the amount of crumpled, used, small-denomination notes that you can carry in one fist at any given time. As a unit of measure, it should be up there with the kilogram or the kilometre, but it has fallen from grace somewhat.

[111] Heh.

[112] I am left wondering if this would work on a commuter-train now. We don't have separate carriages, but someone might think twice about sitting next to me if I start to suck on a rectal thermometer and waggle my eyebrows at them. It might just get me thrown off the train... not being the 14th Baron Berners, and all.

[113] Because that would have been chilly, and nobody wants flying bugs up their bits.

[114] This is probably a bad example. I'd likely take a

few steps back even if someone said that to me in this somewhat more enlightened scientific age.

[115] This is the sort of thing that happens when there's no television. I hate to think how many van Leeuwenhoeks we've lost to Celebrity Love Island and Keeping Up With The Kardashians.

[116] As an aside, the crewmember who pointed the finger at Baltimore was later arrested and hanged for his part in the raid.

[117] I'm not *entirely* sure how this worked. You don't think of having knights on ships, for example, and horses are notoriously not brilliant swimmers. Knights on horseback as the first ironclads doesn't really ring true.

Printed in Great Britain
by Amazon